PHARMAKEIA

A HIDDEN ASSASSIN

Dr. Ana Méndez Ferrell

Voice of The Light Ministries

PHARMAKEIA

A HIDDEN ASSASSIN

Dr. Ana Méndez Ferrell

DEDICATION

In memory of my sister Mercedes Méndez, who was a victim of pharmaceutical science that ravaged her body and caused her death.

In memory of my mother Mercedes Azcárate, who lost her life, as a result of prescription medicine and its side effects destroying her pancreas.

To those who inspired me to live in "Kingdom Health," free from Pharmakeia: My husband Emerson Ferrell, the Apostle Norman Parish and my spiritual son Michaël Scheidegger.

SPECIAL ACKNOWLEDGEMENT

To Julia Schittkowski from Germany, for her love and profound investigation helping the realization of this book.

Voice of The Light Ministries

PHARMAKEIA *A Hidden Assassin*

3rd Edition, Copyright © 2018 Voice of The Light Ministries.

Scripture quotations, are taken from the**King James Version** with Strong's Numbers (in Public Domain), unless otherwise noted.

Category: Deliverance

Published by: Voice of The Light Ministries
                     P.O. Box 3418, Ponte Vedra, Florida 32004 USA
                     www.voiceofthelight.com

Printed in: United States of America

ISBN 978-1-933163-96-3

CONTENTS

Commentaries

Introduction   21

1 God wants to open our eyes   31

2 The mental structures
   of sickness and its cure   39

3 The spiritual aspect of
   conventional medical science   69

4 How the pharmaceutical industry operates   99

5 An organized World System   111

6 The Answer is in God   137

7 God´s fortified Castle   145

8 The Tree of Life & The Wisdom of God   155

9 How to increase our faith
   to stop taking medicine   181

Bibliography

COMMENTARY
by Dr. Jorge Carlos Miranda, M.D., México

RECOMMENDATION TO THE PHYSCIANS
WHO READ THIS BOOK

If you are a health care professional, I recommend the reading of this book, as an additional tool of medical knowledge. I invite you to open your understanding to the revelations of the Spirit of God and begin to walk with steady steps according to His Kingdom. It is difficult to break paradigms; the change is gradual, slow and sometimes incomprehensible, yet I challenge you to grab hold of faith, so you will see the reality of the spriitual world.

MEDICINE IS ART – PHYSICIANS OF THE SPIRIT

Medicine is and can be pointed out, as art and science at the same time. It is the most humane of the arts, the most artistic of the sciences and the most scientific of the humanities. This is the sense we must give to this new medical paradigm: knowing, practice and vocation.

Infirmity encompasses an endless amount of symbols, inherent to every person, whom we as physicians must unveil. Sometimes, we do it through a signal, based on the knowledge of a road of experience that expresses in the symptom, a biography. The reasons for any crisis in the body are of a spiritual and material nature. Only the reflective integration of these natures, apparently contradictory, will allow the attaining of a new model and along with it, the formula to cure the disease of medicine.

Due to the aformentioned, it is necessary for the physician to develop a character that manifests the gifts of the Spirit, because it is written:

For to one is given by the Spirit the word of wisdom; to another the word of knowledge by the same Spirit; to another faith by the same Spirit; to another the gifts of healing by the same Spirit; to another the working of miracles; to another prophecy; to another discerning of spirits; to another divers kinds of tongues; to another the interpretation of tongues

1 Corinthians 12:8-10

An Argentinian physican said the genesis of all diseases is found in the soul (the will, the emotions, reasoning, decisions, choices, and thoughts.)

However, we must recall that the soul is the bridge between the spirit and the body. Through our senses, we can build up, or pollute the spirit and secondly, alter the biologic terrain translating into infirmity.

For we wrestle not against flesh and blood, but against principalities, against powers, against the rulers of the darkness of this world, against spiritual wickedness in high places.

Ephesians 6:12

Medicine is an art, because we can discern infirmity on three fields, (biological, mental and spiritual).

The spirit of man is the candle of the LORD, searching all the inward parts of his being.

Proverbs 20:27

We have to yearn for the spirit of wisdom, intelligence, counsel, power, knowledge and the Fear of God to be able to manifest, among others, the Power of the Spirit through healing.

Finally, I would like to comment that pharmacology is only a small chapter in the formation of a physician, as we count on innumerable non-pharmacological tools to treat the sick. Behind the prescription of any remedy, or treatment, is the devotion, the passion, the empathy, the love, the mercy and the ethics. All these characteristics form, among many others, the physicians task, who sees this profession not just as any job, but instead, as an Apostleship in a minsitry that God has placed in our hearts.

"And these signs shall follow them that believe: In My name shall they cast out devils; they shall speak with new tongues; they shall take up serpents, and if they drink any deadly thing, it shall not hurt them. They shall lay hands on the sick, and they shall recover."

Mark 16:17-18

TO THE READER IN GENERAL

Ana Méndez Ferrells's book is conclusive and revealing, inspired by the Spirit, to be understood by the spirit.

Dr. Jorge Carlos Miranda, M.D.

COMMENTARY
by Dr. René Pelleya-Kouri, M.D., USA

(Author of the Book "Praying Doctors")

Ana Méndez Ferrell has exposed the occult in allopathic medicine. He who has ears, let him hear! This book is not to condemn medicine, but to help us look into higher levels of being in Christ and the divine healing that has already been given to us, by the death and resurrection of Jesus through the cross.

Allopathic medicine helps and at the same time harms many people. Through my years as a practitioner of allopathic medicine, I have a problem with how we tend to look at man simply as a body; a purely mechanical view of man. It does not involve the soul or the spirit. For example, if someone has a headache, we give him a pain pill. If someone is depressed we give him an antidepressant and so on.

I would dare say that the root cause of ALL illnesses lies in the soul and in the spirit. The body gets hit last. A good example of a soul-spirit-psychosomatic illness is fibromyalgia. Many M.D.'s believe there is no real cure for it. People go to psychiatrists, chiropractors, rheumatologists, acupuncturists, pain centers, rehabs and so forth. They take many types of medicines, such as anti-depressants, pain medicine, sedatives, pain modulators and

15

many get worse. But in my practice, every patient that is open for prayer gets healed in one session, just by praying.

There is a hidden world of trauma and unforgiveness in fibromyalgia. There is hurt, resentment, depression, rigidity and a painful syndrome. With spiritual healing and deliverance, there is total healing!

Many illnesses such as migraines, asthma, colitis, arthritis, and the like, respond the same way. Most physicians and most patients, have no idea of this connection between spirit, soul and body. They have not received salvation and are ignorant of the provisions of the cross.

Ana Méndez Ferrell exposes areas of medicine that have roots in non-Christian ways, but the "normal" way of thinking in this society, is mainly rational, intellectual, modern, scientific, materialistic and suchlike. It is not just the medical system, but the whole of this modern society and culture, who lives in denial of the Kingdom of God and the supernatural realms of healing.

The book you hold in your hands dramatically exposes all that could be evil in allopathic medicine. I plan on further exploring and investigating this very interesting topic also.

It also wonderfully shows you how to live in divine health. This, I fully believe and endorse. I recommend this book as an eye opener and as a catalyst for deeper investigation of its contents, but most of all for guiding us to possessing our complete health and wholeness already given to us by God.

Dr. René Pelleya-Kouri, M.D.

PRAYER BEFORE READING THIS BOOK

Heavenly Father, I ask you to open my eyes and my understanding, to see the truths that You want to show me in this book. Allow me that upon reading it, my life and my manner of watching my health to be totally transformed. Give me ears to hear with faith and courage, to decide with determination that I may surrender all my being to You completely to live in the perfect state of health you bought for me at the price of the cross.

"Surely He hath borne our griefs and carried our sorrows; yet we did esteem Him stricken, smitten of God, and afflicted. But He was wounded for our transgressions; He was bruised for our iniquities. The chastisement of our peace was upon Him, and with His stripes we are healed"

Isaiah 53:4-5

INTRODUCTION

I grew up thinking how fortunate we were, those of us who were born in the 20th century, due to the many medical advances.

I marvelled every time there were new discoveries in the field of medical science. My mind simply could not conceive how people in other centuries had lived without today's medicine.

However, my mindset radically changed in 1998, when I saw how the great majority of medications provided to my mother, literaly blew up her pancreas and caused her death.

Later in 2001, my twin sister Mercedes suffered from brain tumors and underwent various surgeries, only to follow my mother's same destiny. The physicians had, in order to prevent a relapse, bombarded her with medication, which in turn destroyed her defense system completely. She ended up dying of a simple cold.

I began to see how medicine, on one hand appeared to do miracles and on the other, it sentenced the population to live even sicker. In the past, people would get sick occasionally, nowadays almost everyone suffers from something for which they have to medicate themselves.

Although it remains true that certain advances in the field of medicine have saved lives, the merchandising of medications has totally corrupted

their humanitarian minds. The apparent advances in medical science have created a dependency on medications, which has not benefitted the people, but is afflicting them with countless ailments as a result of its side effects.

I feel it is my duty on God's behalf, to show society the dangers involved with depending on medication and running to medical science as a first recourse for sickness.

It is not my desire to impose a criteria, nor to condemn anyone. It is my desire that everyone possesses the necessary elements for judgement in order to make correct decisions about their bodies and health.

In the following chapters of this book, you will read terrifying statistics and reports about what happens in the pharmaceutical industry that will leave you speechless.

In my native country of México, as well as in many other Latin American countries, medicine is available to anyone who can afford it. Only psychiatric medications are regulated. Self-medication is commonplace, since the pharmacological manual known by pharmacists as the "Vademécum," can easily be acquired. This is the most complete resource on medications, substances, active principles, drug dosage, interactions, international equivalencies, and pharmacetical laboratories.

Secular bookstores in the United States are riddled with thick books, which contain information about every sort of medication on the market.

In Latin American countries, consulting a physician many times ends up being costly both in money and time. This motivates people with non-complex issues to seek the advice of a pharmacist, or read the Vademécum, believing they can get the adequate medication.

In the United States, a great quantity of medicine for simple cases are found at drugstore counters and no medical prescription is required to obtain them. Adding to this is the impressive bombardment through television advertising for medications, creating an imperative need to run to the doctor, because of everything and because of nothing.

Medications form part of a vicious cycle, which as we will see later, are far from helping us, but rather destroying us.

A pharmaholic structure was built-up inside of me since childhood. Like the majority of people, I was born in a hospital. In my case, my life was endangered from the moment I came into this world. I was born weighing only 3.1 pounds (1.41 kgs), because I was birthed with a twin. The first thing I saw in this world when I opened my eyes, was the confines of an incubator and tubes feeding me.

I obviously know about this through information my mother gave me. Since I was very little, I was injected with a great amount of vaccines, and at the slightest symptom of a cold, I was filled with syrups and pills. When I was born in 1954, people had a family physician who would speedily come over to the residence every time he was summoned, even if it was during the late hours of the evening.

As a result, being sick began to be something very pleasant for my developing little soul. I was treated like a queen and the doctor always brought me candy or a small toy, so I would see his services as something both good and fun. I had my parents attention, they didn't scold me, they brought my meals to my bed, I didn't have to go to school, I could watch television all day, or have grandma read me a storybook. To make sickness and dependency even more attractive, my mom made the mistake of buying us the most trendy toy every time my sister or I got sick. As one may logically assume, my sister and I turned into "professional" sick children.

Stealthily, the devil was building up a structure inside of us, which would undeniably lead us into his deadly trap.

Perhaps mine is not a common case, for each one of us has a unique history, but from an early age, we are compelled to depend on medicine without knowing about the terrible consequences that it entails. Filling children up with vaccines is part of the western culture and we never even ask ourselves whether it is good or bad. We assume that since it was done to us and everyone else does it, then it has to be good.

Little by little and after many years of my conversion to Christ, God opened my eyes to the realization of what scientific medicine really is and how far it is from being a solution. It is one of the most significant causes of death and destruction to the body in our times.

This book is a study from years of searching, while I saw my loved ones, my friends, die without having a solution to help them.

Allopathic medicine, the ordinary one with its antibiotics, analgesics, anti-inflamatories and everything else this type of pharmaceutical medicine implies, is designated as Pharmakeia. It is the greek word used for sorcery. Its origin dates back to ancient Alchemy, which was the art of making medications through sorcery.

Pharmakeia is a terrible power of darkness, which we unconsciously welcome, so it can slowly kill us. We give it the power, the authority and many give it the Glory that should only belong to God.

We receive it as if it were sent by God Himself, putting our entire faith in it. We trust physicians so much that in a certain manner, we have turned them into small gods, who rule us with their diagnoses and their advice. It's not that they want to be deemed as such, but it is us who place them in that role.

Pharmakeia, prince of darkness, becomes our hope and we become its slave, bound for life to its cycle of destruction.

In this book, I am unmasking, what I consider, one of our greatest adversaries in this century. You will read things you have never imagined could be true. You will understand the origin of infirmity and how to destroy it with the power of Jesus Christ. In addition, you will understand how to break the bondages to Pharmakeia and the structure you have built in your mind and in your body set up to kill you.

Within these pages, you will also receive the power to live in perfect health. Jesus did not take your infirmity by His stripes in vain, but up to now, you have not known how to put this powerful truth into action.

I want to clarify something before beginning this expositon. I deeply honor all physicians, who from the bottom of their hearts, strive to help their patients and save lives. Their love and passion, which they've used to rescue so many people from death and how they have served society, has been written in the Book of Life. There will always be a place for physicians and God will use them among those who still do not know Him and His healing and delivering power. He will also use them to help those, who in their struggle to seek liberty, have the need for aid due to some kind of emergency.

My prayer is that God raises a new generation of physicians with a "Kingdom of God - understanding" who can heal by His Wisdom. Just as pharmaceutical science seeks substances to medicate with, the Kingdom physicians will seek revelation from the Lord Jesus Christ on how to guide their patients into Kingdom Health. They will show them how to understand their bodies, how to nourish them, how to balance the substances that are deficient in their organisms and they will give them words of wisdom to change their patterns of conduct that make them sick. Of course, these doctors shall have prayer as their main weapon against illness and disease.

Many modern physicians are leaving conventional medicine and are searching for alternative methods of healing. Many of these new alternative forms are contaminated by New Age, or by withcraft itself and do not afford a solution, but others are good and can help us.

I believe that God is bringing a heavenly wisdom and understanding for us to live in health and to bring the sick to total recovery. I believe that God's Kingdom physicians will be the ones who will be at the forefront and many shall run to Christ because of them. I hope this book serves as an inspiration for them and as a platform to conquer a territory still unknown to our society, resulting in them witnessing many miracles at their medical offices.

In some cases it will be necessary that a Kingdom Physician prescribes some type of medicine, but it will be with a deep knowledge about the product and led by the Spirit of God.

For others, medicine is just big business. My prayer is that they too, come to the Truth, the love, and the compassion like on the day that led them to apply for medical school; for them to know the great Physician of Physicians, who holds the keys to heal every disease and infirmity in His hands.

One of the physicians God is raising in this area is Dr. Jorge Carlos Miranda from México. He wrote one of the commentaries in this book, which will serve as an aide to God's Kingdom Physicians.

1

GOD WANTS
TO OPEN
OUR EYES

Cease not to give thanks for you, making mention of you in my prayers. I pray that the God of our Lord Jesus Christ, the Father of glory, may give unto you the spirit of wisdom and revelation in the knowledge of Him, the eyes of your understanding being enlightened, that ye may know what is the hope of His calling, and what are the riches of the glory of His inheritance in the saints,

Ephesians 1:16-18

God wants to open the eyes of our understanding, so we can see and understand the impressive design He created us with, as well as our inheritance.

God created Adam in absolute perfection, in His image and likeness. He made him from the earth, of physical matter, but breathed His Spirit into him so Adam could be a living soul. When God made the first man, He not only made him of matter, but He fashioned him as a triune being consisting of spirit, soul and body. The body cannnot function isolated from the other two components of the invisible world. The three parts of man collectively determine his state of health.

In the beginning of creation, the spirit of man was joined to God, his soul was in a state of innocence and subjected to the leading of the Spirit. As a result of this, the body could live eternally. This order designed by God produced the fruit of perfect health.

When man entered into a state of sin, this order was altered. The soul took over the lordship from the spirit, the mind crowned itself as sovereign, sustained by human knowledge instead of God's and the body suffered the consequences with a gradual deterioration culminating in death.

God had told man not to eat from the tree of good and evil because he would die if he did it.

But of the tree of the knowledge of good and evil, thou shalt not eat of it. For in the day that thou eatest thereof, thou shalt surely die.
Genesis 2:17

And the serpent said unto the woman, 'Ye shall not surely die; for God doth know that in the day ye eat thereof, then your eyes shall be opened, and ye shall be as gods, knowing good and evil.'
Genesis 3:4-5

The body was made by God to be strong, to resist bacteria, parasites, infections, and disruptions of many sorts.

What literally happened was man exchanged God's knowledge, fellowship and power of eternity, for human, natural knowledge. Man accepted the devil's insinuation to become like God and he died spiritually losing access to his Creator. From this point on, his soul, full of this inferior knowledge, would tell him what was good and what was not.

Death entered the entire human race through one man and brought everything that pertains to this empire, sickness, curse, pain, tragedy, obscurity and sin along with it. Everything was once again in disarray and darkness.

Despite all of this, the human body was made with such wisdom that it could heal itself. God had created it with an impressive defense or immunological sytem. The body was resistant to inclement weather, to food which many times is poisonous or deteriorated due to lack of refrigeration and hygiene.

The body was made by God to be strong, to resist bacteria, parasites, infections, and disruptions of many sorts.

God established man to live 120 years after the flood. He set our life span and this is exceeedingly powerful.

And the LORD said, "My Spirit shall not always strive with man, for he also is flesh; yet his days shall be a hundred and twenty years."

Genesis 6:3

And Moses was a hundred and twenty years old when he died; his eye was not dim nor his natural force abated.

Deuteronomy 34:7

During thousands of years, Abraham's descendants had nothing except their own immunological system and God's covenant of blessing which preserved them.

According to a story told by John G. Lake, the famous revivalist of the earliest 1900's, the people of Israel lived without seeing infirmity for 450 years. During this period, the only ones who got sick were King Asa, who consulted a physician and those who went to the Egyptian physicians brought by Solomon when he married pagan women.[1]

*And Asa, in the thirty and ninth year of his reign, was diseased in his feet until his disease was exceeding great. Yet in his disease he **sought not the LORD, but the physicians.***

And Asa slept with his fathers, and died in the one and fortieth year of his reign.

2 Chronicles 16:12-13

---

[1] John G. Lake © 1995, Kenneth Copeland, Kenneth Copeland Publications, Tulsa, Oklahoma, USA, page 454

God had made a covenant of health with his people on Mount Sinai. The word of God spoken by His own mouth blessing His people was an unassailable shield against every infirmity. All the blessings, the Shalom of God, His peace, His prosperity, His health, His strength, His hosts were His covenant of love over His children as long as they did not break it.

King Asa, however, preferred human knowledge above God's covenant and that decision, just like Adam's, led him to death.

That same life and health blessing is over us, in Christ Jesus who defeated death, infirmity, poverty, pain and sin.

For if by one man's offense death reigned by one, much more those who receive abundance of grace and the gift of righteousness shall reign in life by One, Jesus Christ. Therefore as by the offense of one, judgment to condemnation came upon all men, even so by the righteousness of One, the free gift unto justification of life came upon all men. For as by one man's disobedience many were made sinners, so by the obedience of One shall many be made righteous.

Romans 5:17-19

The reality is that on God's behalf we have every possibility to live in perfect health as we appropriate the inheritance Jesus left us.

The blessing of life is upon us in Christ Jesus, who defeated death and infirmity.

According to Ephesians chapter one, the exceeding greatness of the power of God, who resurrected Him from the dead, defeating death and all its empire, is our inheritance as saints of God.

Therefore, if this is true (which it is), Why are millions of Christians sick?

The answer is that we have established certain structures in our minds, which prevent us from appropriating what is ours.

For the weapons of our warfare are not carnal, but mighty through God for the pulling down of strongholds, casting down imaginations and every high thing that exalteth itself against the knowledge of God, and bringing into captivity every thought to the obedience of Christ, and being in readiness to avenge all disobedience when your obedience is fulfilled.

2 Corinthians 10:4-6

Let's take a look now at which thought structures exalt themselves against the knowledge of Christ.

2

THE MENTAL STRUCTURES OF SICKNESSS AND ITS CURE

1. WHAT IS SICKNESS?

According to the dictionary, sickness is an anomaly of the body, or the mind, which causes pain, dysfunction, anxiety, or death to a person. Used in a general form, this term includes wounds, disabilities, disorders, syndromes, infections, symptoms, and deviant behaviors. Literally, an infirmity is the invasion of pathogens.

Science sees infirmity only from a physical point of view. It has to do with pathogenic agents such as viruses, bacteria, or hereditary organic malformations. Accordingly, we are only matter that desintegrates, one day dies and is transformed into dust. When science encounters something it does not understand, or is unable to diagnose it, it calls is psychosomatic. That is to say, the patient manifests symptoms which originate in the mind.

Medical science views the body as something independent from the soul and from the spirit. It denies the existence of the two aforementioned, and it pretends to be the one which holds the ultimate knowledge to treat a malady.

The reality is that the soul, in its corruptible state begins filling up with grudges, depressions, lies it has believed, wounds not healed, sadness, hate, wrath, envy, strife jealousy, idolatry, witchcraft and all the works of the flesh mentioned in the Epistle to the Galatians Chapter 5. These are the ones, which mine the soul and end up sickening the body.

Dr. Jorge Carlos Miranda says regarding this:

"The concept of an infirmity is complex, it has many aspects to consider, world-visions, paradigms that can be transformed, by the socio-historical visions of every individual.

The word infirmity comes from the Latin 'infirmus': weak, feeble, impotent.

The word infirmity comes from the Latin 'infirmus': weak, feeble, impotent, derived from firmus: firm. Therefore, he who is not firm is infirm; a process referring to the loss and alteration of health; based on modern society.

It is relevant to note that there is a confusion between discomfort and infirmity. Discomfort is the person's subjective experience: feeling sick, and the manner of living it out; infirmity, on the other hand, is a scientific category, separate from the sick subject's personal experience, based on medical knowledge. Both can co-exist. A person may feel bad without being sick, as is the case of an alteration in the emotions, or they may be sick without feeling bad, as is the case of incipient metabolic alterations: diabetes, hyperuricemia, hyper-cholesterolemia and the such. Therefore, for physicians to diagnose an illness, they have to separate the pathological aspect from the feeling of discomfort, since this offers a subjective interpretation. This is important, since the discomfort implicates values and beliefs, which interact with ailments such as: fear, hair loss, nerves, upset stomach, among others.

Even though Infirmity has biological roots, it is also defined by social aspects. It is a disorder of the structure and dynamics of the individual. Sickness is the result of the integration of diverse altered orders in man's reality: the psycho-organic, the social, the historic and the personal one.
Medical methodology, thus conceived, is based on the spirit-matter duality (incompatible amongst them), and upon the fragmentation of the body. Such a discipline, reputed as humanist, does not possess the concept of the integral man (spirit, soul, body), and directs its knowledge toward an artificially fragmented body exclusively based on its biological function, an animalized body or a man-machine. This is quite serious when being a discipline, which deals with life, pain, and death, it lacks a philosophical interpretation of these concepts.

In the last century, the practice of medicine was fragmented by creating specialties. In order to evolve, it will have to reintegrate the same fragments it was divided into."

As we saw in the previous chapter and according to God, sickness entered into man as a result of sin and spiritual death. It is established in the kingdom of darkness and it is a part of the works of the devil to kill and destroy.

We are all born into sin and condemned to die. We are born in a state of darkness until we encounter the true light, which is Jesus Christ.

From that point on, it is our right and our obligation to appropriate everything Jesus conquered for us. This does not happen automatically when we convert. We have to bring the "victory of the resurrection" to every part of our being, spirit, soul and body. Everything must enter into the Light of our Messiah.

After Adam's fall, darkness took authority over humanity. satan became the one who has power over death and sickness. Therefore, every infirmity originates in the devil's territory and is spiritual. It eventually is transferred from the invisible world and becomes visible in the natural world.

> Every infirmity originates in the devil's territory, and for that reason is spiritual.

Now, if we understand the origin of infirmity and what gives it substance, we will be able to deal with it with the spiritual weapons God has given us.

Science regards this approach as insanity or religious fanaticism, but it is God who created us and not science.

Darkness, in all its forms, operates over the soul and it is what produces and gives form to infirmity. Darkness, by definition are all the sins, feelings and negative forms of thought that oppose God. But what is darkness? Darkness is essentially the absence of light. Light has substance and power, darkness has no substance.

Putting it in simple terms: When I turn on the lights at home, I do not have to struggle to push darkness out to establish the light. Darkness disappears automatically in the presence of light.

In him was life; and the life was the light of men. And the light shineth in darkness; and the darkness comprehended it not.

John 1:4-5

Light is the TRUTH, and darkness THE LIE, light is life and darkness is death. satan is real, he is a spirit and the father of all lies and has subjected the world to servanthood through the fear of death (Hebrews 2:15). All of his empire is false, a deceit. It is a simulation, which appears to have an existence, yet doesn't. His great power consists of making us believe that something is real when it isn't.

In his book, *"Immersed in Him"*, my husband Emerson talks masterly about satan, as "the great illusionist", the great magician, the maker of fraudulent tricks, which he uses to deceive humanity.

The problem is, as the Lord himself said it:

> Darkness by definition is all form of sin, feelings and negative forms of thought that oppose God.

My people are destroyed for lack of knowledge: ...

Hosea 4:6a

It's the invisible world that rules over the natural world and not the other way around. If we want to see victory in our bodies and in anything else, we need to understand where the root of the problem lies. In attempting to take down a tree, the solution is to lay an axe to the root and not to try to prune its branches.

If thou seest the oppression of the poor, and violent perverting of judgment and justice in a province, marvel not at the matter; for he that is higher than the highest regardeth, and there are higher than they.

Eclessiastes 5:8

We see in this scripture that what is visible in the natural world is due to a spiritual government that is above it.

This means that the one who is over sickness, is the father of all lies, therefore, any sickness is essentially a lie.

It appears real to us in the natural: bacteria, viruses; the apparent deterioration is visible. X-rays, tomographies, and every form of electronic diagnostics show the anomaly, the tumor, or the sickness, but in truth it has no substance and all that it is, is an abominable lie.

A lie loses its power when it is brought to the light. For example, when someone is committing fraud and deceives everybody with his manner of speaking and false documents, everybody believes him at the onset. However, when the lie surfaces to the light and the fraud

> Infirmity is in itself a lie with no substance, but man gives it reality and power.

is exposed, regardless of how much the scammer wants to continue his exploits, he will not be able to deceive anyone further. He lost his power and ability to lead people astray and all his fraudulent structure crashes down.

Infirmity in itself is a lie and is unsubstantial, but man gives it reality and power. It's the mentality that is separate from God and His Word. It's our negative attitudes and the sick and corrupt feelings we use to face life with that sicken us.

Infirmities are rooted in darkness such as: hate, holding grudges, envy, strife, fornication, greed and the like, as well as trusting in man before God.

We must first see ourselves in the light of God's Word and then ask Him to show us what form and level of darkness has a grip on us.

2. The Great Show

When someone walks in the light, in the love and in the truth of Christ, there is no reason for him or her to get sick. However, we see precious people of God still believing the lies the devil intimidates them with.

This is what happens when the devil stages a great "Terrible Sickness Show." He generates outrageous symptoms and delusional images on the diagnostic instruments. He takes the mouth of an eloquent physician, who declares the infirmity, giving it substance with all types of physical arguments.

The patient believes, without a shadow of a doubt, in the diagnosis and the solutions the physician proposes. At that moment the person submits in spirit, soul and body to believe the diagnosis. He feels horrified, he tells all his acquaintances. They in turn come into agreement with the great lie binding him even more.

Surgery is imminent, the physician has said, "THERE IS NO OTHER REMEDY." The poor sick person believes it 100% and repeats these words once and again to himself. With each thought, he gives form and substance to the infirmity within his being. He is fully convinced that the only alternative left, is to be cut up by the scalpel.

> The essence of things is not found in the physical realm but in the spiritual.

Just in case, because he is a man of "faith", he asks God for a miracle after having made the appointment for the surgery and gives Him twenty-four hours to carry it out. He does not change his manner of thinking, he waits passively for the miracle, while he fills his insides with the "almighty words" of the surgeon. When the twenty-four hours are up, he gives glory to God for having provided someone who will fill him up with anesthesia and perform all types of incisions. The pastor prays for him and the church accompanies him in his pain.

satan not only fulfilled his purposes, but is now in absolute possession of that body to inflict every type of medication, which will destroy it´s immunological system and leave behind a series of sequels and side effects. Afterwards, the devil will use this collateral damage to produce the second attack. All this in the midst of Hallelujahs and glories to God.

Let us understand this important point. In the natural world, everything seems real. It isn't the physician who is lying, he is acting and diagnosing what his senses and knowledge tell him is reality. But the truth, the essence of things, is not found in the physical world but in the spiritual.

The reality is that God does not receive the glory when the words out of our mouths have no substance, as we ignore His principles, only to listen to what man has to say. Jehova is the true "ALMIGHTY GOD", who has the answer to all of our sickness.

Consulting Him should always be our FIRST INSTANCE.

3. The power of the Diagnosis vs The Word of GOD

The power we have granted to medical diagnosis is a stronghold we have built up in our insides. It exerts a great dominion when we have to make a decision.

Society, mass media, governments, medical schools, and the pharmaceutical companies have made medical doctors the UNEQUIVOCAL AUTHORITY, who has the last word pertaining to life and death.

We constantly hear, "Consult your physician". The United States is flooded with signs of this kind. To visit a pool, to get a massage, or to go to a spa, engage in any sport, to go on a ride at an amusement park, in short, for anything and everything, the physician needs to be consulted.

They do this to keep themselves from being sued for not advising people of danger. In certain cases, some people need to be more careful than others, but the point I want to make is this: upon being bombarded by this phrase, a thought structure is formed within us, which is very powerful when we have to make a decision regarding our health.

The words of a doctor carry a gargantuan authority, since we have been putting our trust in and dependence on them throughout the centuries. They are the sages and the "pastors" in regard to infirmity and we, their sheep, who follow them wheresoever they lead.

The words of the wise are as goads, and as nails fastened by the master builders, which are given from one shepherd.

Ecclesiastes 12:11

While wearing a smile on their lips they say: "Don't worry, with this medicine we are going to control your sickness and you will feel better," then people get filled with an unbreakable faith and happily exit the doctor's office.

When they say with a serious face: "Unfortunately, you have a very aggressive cancer and there is nothing to be done," or "you need to be operated on as soon as possible," or "if you stop those pills, you will die," or "you can no longer partake in your favorite sport," or "your problem is that you are bi-polar;" these words are sealed with fire into the heart of the patient, building a new stronghold that is very difficult to overcome.

The Bible says:

Death and life are in the power of the tongue, and they that love it shall eat the fruit thereof.

Proverbs 18:21

What we speak, has an extraordinary power to give life, or to destroy.

Jesus said:

It is the Spirit that quickeneth; the flesh profiteth nothing: The words that I speak unto you, they are spirit, and they are life.

John 6:63

The words from a negative diagnosis are also spirit, but they are unto death, a sting which departs not from us, day or night.

They come out of the physician's mouth with the intention of being received as an irrefutable truth. We, along with the rest of society, have conferred them that power.

The Apostle Paul says:

O foolish Galatians! Who hath bewitched you, that ye should not obey the truth, before whose eyes Jesus Christ hath been evidently set forth, crucified among you?

Galatians 3:1

> The words from a negative diagnosis are also spirit, but they are unto death.

The words from a man of authority produce a fascination, which exerts a power above that which God has said. Adding the spirit of sorcery to this, knowing *Pharmakeia* is seeking to throw its hook into the doctor's office to catch the unwary, how great a seduction does this end up being?

Why don't we begin by saying, "Consult God", instead of "consult your physician?" Will God have something more powerful to say than what medical science says? He who made man with all His love, can He not cure him? Of course He can!

God does not want to eliminate the physicians, He wants to re-educate us and them, putting His consciousness in our way of thinking.

The problem lies in the fact that many are unable to seize the promises and the power of God to live in the health of His Kingdom. We believe that if we are not healed at the healing crusade, or after the pastor has prayed for us, then there is nothing else to do but to run to *Pharmakeia*. This is false.

God wants to open our eyes to see and understand how we can get healed and live in divine health. If you are a physician, God wants to teach you how to become one working on behalf of the Kingdom of God.

Now, allow me to shed some light regarding what happens within us, long before

> God does not want to eliminate the physicians.
> He wants to reeducate us and them, putting His consciousness in both.

making a critical decision about a surgery, or accepting a chronic or lethal illness, or deciding whether to take medication.

4. The Structure of Infirmity inside us

As I explained in the Introduction, from childhood we begin forming ideas and mental structures that determine our behavior. These strongholds are anti-scriptural and will surface at the moment we have to make a drastic decision.

From childhood, we begin to program our minds, by what we continually hear. In the case of ailments, the sequence is: Infirmity = run to the doctor = receive a diagnosis = solution = take medication, and worst case scenario: get hospitalized.

We learn this sequence from our parents, from our teachers at school, from family and friends, at church, on TV, at the movies, from billboards and during political campaigns. It's everywhere! It's what the majority thinks and believes and therefore has become the national and world frame of mind.

In the United States alone, 60 % of television advertisements are about diseases and medications.

It is such a powerful stronghold that it is very difficult to break. It seems so logical. It is accepted by society, governments and the church. We constantly hear about this cycle from one person to the next. In the United States alone, 60 % of television advertisements are about diseases and medications, 15 % about junk food, which inevitably leads to getting sick and many others about insurance companies who offer to pay for medicine and hospitalization.

We are bombarded everywhere, by a thought-and-action-pattern, which has trapped the majority of the people including the sons of God.

As potential patients, we are not the only ones who have been forming this mind structure, but the medical schools are to be blamed as well. From the time a med student enters a university, he is powerfully convinced that THE ONLY WAY TO CURE SICKNESS IS THROUGH SCIENCE. He hears a million times, "There is no other way", "Life and death are in your hands", "You are the solution, along with the instruments and the drugs science will put in your hands". These institutions create within each of their students the concept that everyone is necessarily ill, or will be, at any given moment. They are trained for years at a medical school, to see infirmity only and exclusively from a physical point of view and from a humanist philosophy, which tells them: Man and his medical advances are THE ONLY SOLUTION. They are conditioned to believe, to live and to perpetuate a system of infirmity.

Dr. Ghislaine Lanctot writes in her book *"The Medical Mafia"*[2]:

---

[2] *The Medical Mafia*, Dr. Ghislaine Lancot @ 1995 Bridge of Love Publications, U.K.

"The so-called sanitary method is in reality a system of infirmity. A medicine of infirmity is practiced, not one of health, a medicine that only acknowledges the existence of the physical body and does not take into account neither the spirit, the mind, nor the emotions. And besides, it only treats the symptom and not the cause of the problem. It's about a system, which keeps the patient in ignorance and dependency and who is stimulated to consume pharmaceutical products of every sort."

The medical boards, councils and groups, medical and pharmaceutical congresses create in doctors' minds such structures that even for them, it's "the unswerving truth." They are conditioned to never, ever question themselves, whether what they have learned is, or isn't approved by God.

I myself, even heard preachers say so many times: *"Medicine is of God, because the devil has no interest in healing anybody."* What brilliant thinking, I thought for so many years! And it would be true, if healing was the response and its fruits were a healthier society evermore. *"You shall know them by their fruits."*

> Never has a society been as sick and with so many new ailments as ours.

Unfortunately, they are producing quite the contrary. Our generations are sick from birth and even from the mother's womb. Never has a society been as sick and with so many new ailments as ours.

Something is very wrong and begins with our thought patterns regarding infirmity. People are not born, grow up with and develop a "full health"-mind set, one of strength, of vigor, and longevity. Our cultures are polluted by erroneous thoughts contrary to God. They have filled us with fear of sickness, fear of the unexpected, and of death. They have people, Christians included, spinning in a death cycle from which they have to be set free.

An article published by Dr. Joseph Mercola says the following:

"... as has been repeatedly demonstrated and as can be seen in the last list of high risk medications published by the FDA (Food and Drug Admintration) the pharmaceutical industry is NOT producing magic elixirs for Good Health. On the contrary, the industry is gaining power and strength propagating sickness without providing its cure.

Unfortunately, treating the symptoms of the infirmity with medication will invariably create health issues, which leads to taking more drugs to counteract the side effects from the first one and then another and another more. It's a wicked cycle, when the statistics of medicine prescribed per person is analyzed, which have exponentially increased in the last 75 years.

In 1929, the average American was prescribed 2 medications per year; by the year 2006 the average rate of prescribed medication per person in United States was:

- *more than 4 medicines per child (Ages 10-18)*
- *almost 11 medicines per adult   (Ages 19-64) and*
- *28 medicines per adult in their senior years (over 65)"*

By 2009, the average per person consumption in America was between 12 and 18 medications.[3]

This is without counting the innumerable pills and syrups obtained over the counter, which would increase the list by 100 to 200 percent up, more or less; this being a conservative estimate.

In Latin America, these numbers are unfathomable given the free administration of medications, which do not require a medical prescription.

If these medicines would produce a healthy society, every year they would become less indispensable and our countries would enjoy better health.

By 2009, the average per person consumption in America was between 12 and 18 medications.

We have to realize that both physicians, as well as patients, have been enveloped in a cycle of destruction, which is not benefitting anybody except the pharmaceutical companies.

[3] http://www.statehealthfacts.org

Today, we have infirmities, which did not exist before and which are the result of the tons of harmful chemicals our society consumes.

Thus, sickness does not only come from sin and generational iniquity, but also from a system of addiction, which has destroyed the bodies of those who have consumed them, of their children and their grandchildren and so on.

A structure of manipulation

Another thought structure, which produces sickness is when people use their infirmity to manipulate someone else. This can happen to get a mate's attention, or that of the children, or of the parents.

There are people who, because of not having resolved their low self esteem and rejection issues, literally create sicknesses, which manifest in their bodies to control their loved ones. It's like a self-defense mechanism, which is totally erroneous and destructive.

How many times have we heard of mothers who become ill to keep their children tied to them, manipulating them with phrases such as this one: "How dare you leave me here sick and alone!"

Unresolved sentimental problems create a great deal of heart diseases, which in turn, are used to create guilt in the spouse and to punish him (her) in this manner.

The solution is not chemicals or drugs, but to go to the root of the problem and solve it.

When I was a little girl, I saw that every student who came to school with an arm or a leg in a cast turned into the classroom hero. Everybody would gather around them. The casts were almost like a trophy teeming with signatures and drawings, which children would treasure as a big deal. Of course, I wanted to break a bone and if I were lucky enough to be hospitalized that would place me on the highest pedestal to captivate everybody's attention.

Of course, I attained it. I never broke anything, but when I was operated on for appendicitis, I felt like I had won the lottery.

In middle and high school, getting sick was a marvelous escape from all my obligations. Thank God I never got sick from anything gravely serious. Yet, inside me, a deep deformity in my way of thinking was being shaped. For me, just like for the majority, physicians were like "saviors", a refuge to run to, somebody marvelous, full of solutions, a godlike beings who had all the answers.

Though all of this sounds like a joke, it is a reality that is built up in our minds through different circumstances, excuses, and reasoning. Some, as dumb and infantile like my case, and others having a more formidable foundation.

A preconceived sickness mentality

People create a mental panorama of everything they will undergo in life. If there is a family disease such as cancer, diabetes, or some serious illness, people begin to predispose themselves to get said diseases. Every time they go to the physician, they are asked if there is a history of any of these ailments in the family. The doctor, as well as the patient, are convinced that the dormant infirmity will one day appear.

What I want you to realize is how we create a mental idea and a thought structure that will inevitably be used by the devil to destroy us.

Our fallen nature is made to believe, what science and physicians say, placing it above what God says. We have to shatter it to pieces, so the new creature in Christ Jesus, can emerge, otherwise our own thoughts will give "a way and life" to disease.

I continuosly hear these statements: "when we get to such and such an age, the bones become laden with osteoporosis", "menopause is terrible, it produces depression because of a lack of hormones", "teeth fall out at a certain age", "this produces cancer, and this other thing does too", "the flu season is coming, do not go out without covering yourself otherwise you will get pneumonia" and "if I don't take this medicine, this and that is going to happen to me." All of them verbalize something tragic.

These, as well as hundreds of other statements condition the mind to make us prone to that which we fear, may happen to us.

The fear of the wicked, it shall come upon him; but the desire of the righteous shall be granted.

Proverbs 10:24

All of these thoughts are ungodly, they are not from God, nor do they come from the Mind of Christ.

I was absolutely convinced that unless I medicated myself, I was unable to survive. I lived believing all these things as if they were the immutable truth, only because science and many physicians believe it to be so.

The good thing is that God does not think like this.

For I know the thoughts that I think toward you, saith the LORD, thoughts of peace and not of evil, to give you an expected end. Then shall ye call upon Me, and ye shall go and pray unto Me and I will hearken unto you. And ye shall seek Me and find Me when ye shall search for Me with all your heart.
Jeremiah 29:11-13

The important question we must ask ourselves while facing such a bombardment from medicine and from our own structures is:

Can science heal that which it did not create?

As we already saw, science can only pretend to heal matter, our physical bodies, disassociating them from our mental, emotional and spiritual reality.

This is like trying to fix a car that doesn't run dealing only with the bodywork.

Our being, is a complex apparatus, marvelously connected between its three main components: Body, soul and spirit.

Our Creator is the only one who has the blueprints of such engineering genius. He is the only One Who understands how physical matter interrelates to the invisible body of the spirit, and how these are joined by an invisible third component called the soul. The natural man, with all its wisdom and science, is incapable of even conceiving this triune architecture.

Let the wicked forsake his way and the unrighteous man his thoughts; and let him return unto the LORD, and He will have mercy upon him, and to our God, for He will abundantly pardon. For My thoughts are not your thoughts, neither are your ways My ways, saith the LORD. **For as the heavens are higher than the earth, so are My ways higher than your ways and My thoughts than your thoughts.**

Isaiah 55:7-9

And God also says about His wisdom and that of men:

Because the foolishness of God is wiser than men, and the weakness of God is stronger than men. For ye see your calling, brethren, how that not many wise men after the flesh, not many mighty, not many noble, are called: But God hath chosen the foolish things of the world to confound the wise; and God hath chosen the weak things of the world to confound the things which are mighty;

1 Corinthians 1:25-27

Allegorical painting by Alexander Egorovich Beideman (1857) showing the horror with which Homeopathy and Samuel Hahnemann view the medicine of that time period.

A human being trying to heal, what is a divine design, is the same as a six year old child trying to repair the electronic and mechanical systems of a Boeing 787 Jet. The only thing the kid would succeed at is joining two cables and rejoicing over the little sparks it made as it broke down the systems.

This analogy sounds cruel, but unfortunately, it is a reality; always acknowledging that in "certain cases," they have hit the bull's eye and achieved healing.

As detailed earlier, the need to ingest medication progressively increases in our society. Every year our nations are sicker than the year before.

According to a study done by doctors *Gary Null, Carolyn Dean, Martin Feldman, Debora Rasio* and *Dorothy Smith*, 783,936 people die every year in the United States because of mistakes made by conventional medicine. This is equivalent to six Jumbo Jets crashing daily for a year.

If we add the amount of people who die due to medical errors, to those who pass away due to side effects of prescription medicine, and the mortality due to self-prescription and medication abuse, we find a number which is **104,700 percent** higher than those who die from terrorism.[4]

---

[4] summary segment from the report "Death by Medicine" by Gary Null, PhD, Carolyn Dean, MD, ND Martin Feldman, MD, Debora Rasio, MD, Dorothy Smith, PhD.

These statistics lead us to conclude that many of the famous, great advances in medicine are not helping humanity, but destroying it.

I am not saying this to state there is absolutely no place for medicine. There are obvioulsy cases in which a surgery or the aid of paramedics, who have saved so many lives, is necessary. Of course, if somebody needs to be sutured, or put in a cast, or whatever is required because he (she) suffered an accident, a heart attack or something similar, the physicians need to treat him. Also, if childbirth puts the mother or the baby at risk, a c-section will be indispensable, and likewise procedures in other cases.

What God wants us to realize, is what the pharmaceutical industry is doing to humanity and the abuses and aberrations they have reached with the marketing of medicine. Sickness has turned into something generalized. In expectation of selling more products, they have created what is known as preventive medicine and the risk factor. They try to fill us up with pharmaceutical products, because we may potentially generate a malady. In this fashion, they ensure that everyone becomes their client. Statistics show that 81 percent of the population in the western world is on medication.

In the United States 783,936 people die every year because of mistakes made by conventional medicine.

The multiplication of drugstores in Latin America is impressive. We can find them everywhere. There are zones in which there is a drugstore on every block. Just take a look at the border cities.

In the United States and in Latin America, the majority of the great supermarkets have a pharmacy attached.

This is not the design of God for His children. Neither has God placed His solutions on the wise of this world.

Regardless of how much man may eat of the tree of science of good and evil, with his limited knowledge he will never be able to fix a body that has become ill without damaging it in the attempt. This is found solely in the faculty of He who made it and knows how our integral organism functions.

God wants to raise up men and women full of His knowledge and His science to help the disabled and those needy of health. Doctors of health **possessing at the same time** the knowledge of life, anointed to heal and to orient the people of God and the world on how to live in "Divine Health."

As we advance in this study, solutions will dawn on you and on the blessings God has prepared for you.

What I first want to do is to give you light, so you can see the structures of destruction and death, which are not helping you at all.

Light comes to give understanding and revelation and not to condemn anybody. The intention of my heart is to show you the exit door from infirmity and give you answers to your needs. Each one shall make the decisions according to their faith and according to their case.

Remember, the thoughts of God are of continuous good for your life. He wants to see you healthy and full of strength to carry out the work He has charged you with.

Let's now take a look back in history and see where *Pharmaceutical* or *Pharmakeia* in its original name comes from and what God thinks about those who practice it.

3

THE SPIRITUAL ASPECT OF CONVENTIONAL MEDICAL SCIENCE

1. PHARMAKEIA – A Power of Darkness

Pharmakeia is the name of a power of darkness rooted amongst mankind since ancient Egypt. It's the spirit of sorcery, witchcraft and occultism, which arose from that empire. The Greek word *Pharmakeia*, is translated as sorcery and magic in our Bibles. From its root, *"Pharmakon"*, which means: Poison, drug, medication, come the words *pharmacy*, *pharmaceuticals*, *drug*, and *drug addiction*. *"Pharmakos"* is also the word used for sorcerer, or warlock.

*Blessed are they that do His commandments, that they may have right to the Tree of Life, and may enter in through the gates into the city. For without are dogs and **sorcerers**, **(pharmakos** -5332 in Strongs) and whoremongers and murderers and idolaters, and whosoever loveth and maketh a lie.*

Revelation 22:14-15

Just like a spell or magic potion, the spirit of pharmakeia seeks to bind men up and to make them addicted to a system that will enslave them for life. As we just read in the previous passage, those who are trapped in that system, cannot enter the powerful dimensions of the Kingdom of God.

Somebody can attain salvation while being bound to medication; but will never enjoy the health and the benefits God gave him or her as an inheritance.

I was rescued from witchcraft and occultism, but I would never have had the authority God has now given me over this spirit, if I hadn't first vanquished every bondage from pharmakeia.

Many want to have authority over sorcery, set the captives free from witchcraft, from drug addiction, while they themselves, are bound to the chains of pharmakeia.

They are suffering because their children are prisoners to drugs and they pray for them from the very prison cells of pharmaco-dependency.

This is much more serious than can be imagined and what you are going to read subsequently, will make you realize that pharmakeia cannot heal. Not only does it lack the power to accomplish healing, but the devil's will to do it as well.

Pharmakeia seeks to bind men up and to make them addicted to a system that will enslave them for life.

Rather, Pharmakeia is a weapon of destruction, a time bomb that sooner, or later, will wreak havoc. If perhaps, some medicine gave you the fleeting illusion of health, the price will

be deeply entrenched in your cells and some day it will surface and you'll pay for it.

The solution lies in the knowledge of God through His son Jesus Christ, Who truly knows the blueprints of our organism.

Pharmakeia does not operate alone, it's intimately related to "*Mammon*, the god of riches" and as we will see, its origin emerges from man's desire to produce gold.

Today, the pharmaceutical industry around the world generates close to a trillion dollars annually and is part of an organized system, which controls a great part of humanity.

2. Pharmakeia in History

It's important to understand the genesis of medicine in order to discern the spiritual background which surrounds it. It's in the origin of everything man has done, where the powers of darkness have been entrenched to influence a society. It's at that point where the master covenants were made to invoke those demonic forces. If the origin is not changed, regardless of how many transformations a practice or a science undergoes, its spiritual aspect continues to be the same.

Pharmakeia is a weapon of destruction, a time bomb.

Modern allopathic medicine has its origin in ancient "Alchemy" (from the Arab *al-khimia*). This is an ancient protoscientific practice and philosophical discipline, which combines elements from chemistry, metallurgy, physics, medicine, astrology, semiotics, mysticism, spiritualism, and art. Alchemy was practiced in Mesopotamia, Ancient Egypt, Persia, India and China, also in Ancient Greece, the Roman Empire, the Islamic Empire, and later, in Europe until the 19th Century. It formed a complex network of schools and philosophic systems, which spanned at least 2,500 years.[5]

Western Alchemy has always been related to *Hermetism*, a philosophical and spiritual system, which has its roots in *Hermes Trimegisto*, a Greek-Egyptian deity and also in his human form, one of the greatest occultists. In modern times, Alchemy evolved into the current chemistry, but the spirits that enacted its origin, continue to control it. Hermes, along with the group of pagan gods who sustain the alchemist and pharmacological system, carry great importance among occultists.

Alchemy was one of the main forerunners of modern science and many of the substances, tools and processes of ancient alchemy have served as fundamental pillars to the modern chemical and metallurgical industries.

Although alchemy adopts many forms, in popular culture, it is represented with greater frequency in stories, movies, television shows and games as the process used to

---

[5] http://en.wikipedia.org/wiki/alchemy

transform lead (and other elements) into gold. Another aspect of Alchemy is the search for the Philosopher's Stone, with which they aimed to transmute gold, or obtain eternal life.[6]

In the spiritual plane of alchemy the alchemists had to transmute their own souls before transmuting the metals. This meant they had to purify themselves, prepare through meditation and specific rituals to obtain the power to transmute matter.

The love of riches and the search for it, were the foundations of alchemy and currently of the pharmaceutical industry. It´s goals were:

1. Find a *"Panacea"*, a universal remedy against all sicknesses.

2. Find the *"Philosopher's Stone"*.

3. Find the *"Alkahest"*, a universal solvent based on potassium carbonate. (this where the name for the common remedy *Alka-Seltzer* comes from)

3. Alchemy as a spiritual and philosophical discipline.

The alchemists upheld that the Philosopher's Stone, if it was used in a mystical way, would amplify the knowledge of the one who used it. It contained wisdom within itself to

---

[6] http://en.wikipedia.org/wiki/Philosopher's_stone

ıe universal panacea (medication) and gold. But,
e was this?

In its spiritual form it was the manifestation of
***Basilisk*; a winged dragon with the head and the feet of a**
rooster.

The Basilisk is known
as the god of healing

Alchemists searched for this dragon, because they believed its ashes mixed with human blood and reddish hair could create the anti-venom (medication) as well as gold. The basilisk was known in its spiritual form as the **king of the serpents**. From thereon we will always find serpents associated with medicine. It's not by happenstance that satan, incited the first couple to eat from the tree of good and evil using the form of a serpent.

Since 1448, many figurines and statues of dragons and basilisks can be found in the city of Basel in Switzerland. It is not by coincidence that today this is one of the most important centers of the world pharmaceutical industry; among them are the laboratories of Ciba, Novartis, Roche, Basilea Pharmaceutical, Acino Holding also known as Syngenta.

The Basilisk and the Philosopher's Stone were one and the same. The god of healing who promised gold and medication.

The serpent, as well as the rooster, are symbols of betrayal and death.

The serpent only needs to "inject" the venom into its victim and afterwards leaves. It is an attack to the inside of the body, silent, almost unnoticed, that slowly and painfully leads to death.

The rooster, as was the case of the Apostle Peter, is linked to treason, the betrayal of Jesus. It's an announcer of an evil that can no longer be remedied and brings torment to the soul: depression. The serpent attacks the body, the rooster the mind; a couple designed to destroy.

During the Middle Ages, some alchemists gradually began to treat metaphysics as the authentic foundation of Alchemy. They considered chemical substances, physical states, and material processes as sheer metaphors for entities, states and spiritual transformations. This way, the transmutation of ordinary metals into gold, as the universal panacea, symbolized the evolution from an imperfect, sick and corrupt state into a perfect, healthy, incorruptible, and eternal state. The Philosopher's Stone, or Basilisk represented the mystical key that would make this evolution possible.[7]

The serpent is the traditional symbol of medicine.

---

[7] http://en.wikipedia.org/wiki/alchemy

The most important name during this period was *Paracelsus* (1493–1541). Together with the alchemists of his time, Paracelsus tried to produce live entities inside a test-tube. He called these artificial entities "Homunculus" (little human) or Basilisk. These entities frequently appeared as demonic helpers to facilitate the alchemist practices.

The formula to create it appears among the writings of Paracelsus. It was a combination of human sperm and blood with horse dung along with other ingredients, which after letting it stand for 40 days, created a sort of a very small transparent child. Paracelsus declared: *"Magic is a great hidden science and reason, an open foolishness."*

Homunculus

Paracelsus was the pioneer in the use of chemical and mineral compounds in medicine. He wrote: *"Many have said of Alchemy that it is for the making of gold and silver. For me, such is not the aim, but to consider only **what virtue and power may lie in medicines.**"*[8] His hermetical points of view were that sickness and health of the body depended on man's harmony (microcosm) with nature (macrocosm).

However, Paracelsus took a different approach than his predecessors, using this analogy, not as a reference to the purification of the soul, but as an argument supporting thesis that human must maintain certain mineral equilibriums in his body and that there are chemical remedies that could cure certain infirmities.[9]

4. ALCHEMY IN GREECE
THE BASIS OF PRESENT DAY MEDICINE

Alchemy in Greece is one of the most important fundamentals of present day medicine. The great philosophers, thinkers, and scientific inventors in the West came from this culture.

Greece was greatly influenced by the magic and the alchemy of Egypt and among their mythologies some of the gods are analogous. It is worth noting that the first identifiable figure in medicine in Ancient Egypt was

---

[8] The Dark Side of History, Michael Edwardes © 1977 Stein and Day, New York, page # 47
[9] Alchemy and Chemistry in the Seventeenth Century, Allen G. Debus & Robert P. Multhauf © 1966, William Andrews Clark Memorial Library, University of California, Los Angeles, pages # 6-12

Imhotep. He was a physician, an architect, a statesman, and a musician. He lived until the year 2950 B.C. and it was because of him that not far from Cairo, the *Pyramid of Saqqarah* was built, which today is the most ancient stone structure existent on the planet.

The Greek city of Alexandria in Egypt, was an alchemic center of wisdom that retained its preeminence during the greater part of the Greek and Roman eras. Greeks appropriated the Egyptian hermetic beliefs and united them with their philosophies. That's how Hermes was formed, the god of Science, Communication, Alchemy and Chemistry.[10]

Hermes

---

[10] http://en.wikipedia.org/wiki/alchemy

Hermes is the one in charge, by the gods, to take **the souls of dead to Hades (hell).** He carries a magic wand with two coiled serpents in his hand. With this wand he puts people to sleep and brings them dreams.

Today, under the same symbol, people are taken into the captivity of sickness, pharmaco-dependency and led to death.

The word "*Caduceus*" comes from the Greek root word, which means the "small rod of a herald" or "staff". Both the rod of *Mercury* (Latin name of Hermes), as well as the staff of *Asclepius* (Aesculapius), which we will see further on, were born from the worship of the serpent.

Caduceus

Among the Egytpians the serpents were the Pharaoh's tomb keepers, since they guarded the doors to the underworld.

Egyptian Serpent in the underworld

The Emerald Tablet, or Hermetic, from Hermes Trismegistus (only known through Greek and Arab translations), is normally considered the basis of philosophy and western alchemic practices, called by its first followers Hermetic philosophy.

Janes and Jambres, the magicians whom Moses confronted in Egypt, were this type of Alchemists.

And Moses and Aaron went in unto Pharaoh, and they did so as the LORD had commanded; and Aaron cast down his rod before Pharaoh and before his servants, and it became a serpent. Then Pharaoh also called the wise men and the sorcerers. Now the magicians of Egypt, they also did in like manner with their enchantments. For they cast down every man his rod, and they became serpents; but Aaron's rod swallowed up their rods.

Exodus 7:10-12

It's interesting to note that the most important deliverance of the people of Israel begins with a confrontation with the Egyptian alchemists, in other words, with Pharmakeia.

Ever since then, God has been saying: *"My solutions devour the serpents of alchemy. My power is greater than that of* **Pharmakeia***."*

Later in the scriptures, the Alchemists again enter Israel during the time of Solomon, when his various ungodly wives have them brought forth, and they once again open the doorway to sickness. The most grandiose empire of peace, health and prosperity was contaminated and sits downfall occurs from thereon.

By now, it starts to become evident how the serpents and the gods, which represent them, are intimately related to sustain and to promote the work of Pharmakeia. One more entity added to this list is satan himself, under the name of *Aeskulap* or *Asclepius* (Aesculapius). His scepter is the actual symbol of the Pharmaceutical field.

This is the god of medicine in Greek mythology. It was said that he always had a serpent coiled on his rod.

Aesculapius (Asclepius)

The cult of Asclepius was established in the 5th Century B.C. and it was one of the most relevant ones of the ancient world.

In Mythology all the gods, apart from causing sickness and death, also cured the infirmities and healed the wounds. In Ancient Greece, like in Egypt, religious medicine became firmly established. The priests in their temples and sanctuaries desired to satisfy human needs. Infirmity in Ancient Greece could be treated by gods and semi-gods who practiced the art of healing.

Apollo had under his responsibility health, medicine, bodily and spiritual purification and was also the god of singing and hexametric verse. Initially, Apollo used to be the most important, but was sequentially eclipsed by his son Asclepius (Asclepius, Aeskulap), who transformed during the latter third of the fifth century A.D. from a lesser hero to a higher god.

The worship of Asclepius and modern day medicine

The temple of Asclepius is a prototype of modern day hospitals. According to various historians, the worship of Asclepius took place in the following manner:

First, the sick were bathed in one of the many temple pools and then they had to pay a fee to *Apollon* (Apollo).

At nightime, they laid down in beds inside some special tunnels called *"Clines"*. From this Greek word, the word "Clinic" is derived. These rooms were destined for a therapeutical sleep called *incubation*. The temple servants, called *therapists* in Greek, would turn off the light and ask for silence. A priest started with picking up the bread of oblation from the altar. Afterwards, the god Asclepius, escorted by his two daughters and a slave, would go from bed to bed to examine the sick, mix ointments and syrups.

Among the daughters was *Hygiea*, the goddess of "health", *Aceso* that of recovery; *Laso* and *Panacea*, the goddess who cured everything, goddess of medication. His wife *Epione* (the sweet) accompanied them sometimes with their sons *Podaleirios* and *Machaon*.

For the sick, as well as for the priests who came into contact with Asclepius, the method for the cure was revealed in the dreams. Some dreamt that Asclepius's serpent would bite them and then they could be healed.

The sick would then speak to a temple priest, who analyzed the method of cure. During the whole time of the treatment, the patient would stay in a guest room. As a part of the therapy, they had theatre and entertainment.

Temple of Asclepion

The famous hospital of the ancient world, dedicated to the god of health, Asclepius, "The Asclepion" is 3.5 km away from the center of *Pergamum*, heading toward *Smyrna*. This is where the famous physician *Galenus* lived, who was the father of modern medicine. The physicians of that time, were known as disciples of *Saint Asclepius*.

This temple in Pergamum is the one referred to in the Book of Revelation as the "throne of satan."

*Write this letter to the angel of the church in Pergamum. This is the message from the one with the sharp two-edged sword: I know that you live in the city where **satan has his throne,** yet you have remained loyal to me.*

Revelation 2:12-13a NLT

According to Jesus Christ himself, who has revealed this to John, this temple, the prototype of present day hospitals, is called the temple of satan. I am not saying that hospitals are temples of satan, but I do not deny his presence in them.

Asclepius had a daughter named *Hygeia* (Greek word which means health). She is the goddess of health and patroness of the pharmacologists. The word "hygiene" is also derived from her name. Her sister *Panacea* is the goddess of medication and sorcery. From the latter comes the word panacea, the elixir that cures all.

Asclepius dealt with healing while Hygeia dealt with the prevention of sickness. She was worshipped from 700 B.C. and after the plague that swept Athens in 430 B.C., her worship was extended all the way to the city of Delphi.

Hygeia

Her image is always accompanied by a serpent coiled to her arm drinking from a bowl. This symbol is everywhere in hospitals and pharmacies, together with that of Asclepius. To further certify her relationship with occultism, in some countries such as Germany, a druid rune was added to the pharmaceutical symbol.

Serpent with bowl

Hygeia with Asclepius

Now, let's see the influence of all these gods and their spells on modern day medicine.

4.1 OATH OF HIPPOCRATES

Hippocrates was born in 460 AD and came from the generational line of *Aesclepiades*, a follower of Asclepius, the god of health.

He is considered the father of medicine, of science and the founder of the first school for physicians.

In the majority of medical schools, the *Oath of Hippocrates*[11] is the first law the graduate from these institutions has to abide by. It is considered a tradition and part of the graduation ritual.

In the majority of medical schools, the *Oath of Hippocrates* is the first law the graduate has to abide by.

In Christian universities and in some of the Catholic ones, this has been substituted by a more contemporary oath.

The Oath begins in the following manner:

"I swear by Apollo, the healer, Asclepius, Hygieia and Panacea, and I take to witness all the gods, all the goddesses, *to keep according to my ability and my judgment, the following Oath and agreement ...*

... **I will not give a lethal drug to anyone if I am asked,** *nor will I advise such a plan; and similarly I will* **not give a woman a pessary to cause an abortion."**

And it culminates with:

"... If I keep this oath faithfully, may I enjoy my life and practice my art, respected by all men and in all times; but **if I swerve from it or violate it, may the reverse be my lot."**

---

[11] Although the oath has been changed in many nations the spiritual reality behind it remains the same

In this oath, the new medical graduate has to lay down his career, swearing by satan himself. And should he break the pact, or if he has converted to God, he immediately becomes subjected to a curse.[12]

He swears not to give anyone a lethal drug, when medicine per se, is a poison. Remember, the origin of the word *Pharmakos* means poison, bewitchment, witchcraft. Later, I will expand upon in detail, the abominations of modern day chemistry and how allopathic medicine kills and destroys instead of curing.

Many physicians are in agreement that allopathic medicine, in general, has its different levels of risks. Those who have abandoned this type of medicine have arrived at the conclusion that it cannot cure anybody, but only encapsulate or diminish the symptom. They also know that its side effects destroy the body's immunological system and in many cases, it becomes terribly aggressive toward the vital organs causing death in many patients.

Now there are medicines and treatments, which in very particular cases, do marvels in a short period, but the majority of the physicians don't know the consequences they will bring in the long run. There are no laboratories that wait 20 years, doing experimental trials on a medication before putting it out on the market.

---

[12] In some nations this oath ceased to be used in this form in the year 1948 – decision of World Medical Association. No god is invoked. It was further changed in 1968, 1983, 1994 and finally in 2005 altered to allow abortion and euthanasia.

Even the laboratories themselves know that every body reacts differently and that it would be impossible to predict the reactions of each individual.

The majority of physicians are unaware of the contents of many medications and the test-results the chemists faced at these labs.

They also know that medical science being so fragmented into so many specialties, the interchanging of chemical substances prescribed by doctors, who have no relationship with one another, increases the risk of side effects and unexpected reactions.

I recently read an article published by Dr. Mercola, denouncing the medications that the FDA (Food and Drug Administration) considered as "high risk". He stated:

"Do not believe for a minute that physicians have all the answers and the latest pharmaceutical investigations at the tip of their tongue. They don't. The majority of the physicians have little to offer above the advertisement they read in the pamphlet from the lab sales representative."

In her book *"The Truth About Drug Companies"*, Marcia Angell writes about the ways in which the pharmaceutical manufacturing companies distort the flow of information on the risks and benefits of the medications that reach the physicians.

In this book, she contends that the majority of information physicians possess about medicines is received through the pharmaceutical company representatives. In general, these are attractive young women without any medical or scientific background. As a matter of fact, the way the New York Times states it in their November 28, 2005 edition, is that these companies enlist young, female university students who are leading cheerleaders at football games. The article is called: *"Gimme an Rx! Cheerleaders Pep Up Drug Sales."*[13]

Now going back to the *Hippocratic Oath:* The physician took an oath that he would not give any lethal drug to anyone, in some cases inviting as witnesses, the gods of hell, and at the same time, being unaware of the true risks of the medicine he prescribes.

On the other hand, he swears to never give an abortive, when a large amount of birth control pills are abortive methods, apart from other medications that they know about, or are unaware of.

Because of many reasons, the physician ends up bound to the curse, while he diagnoses, operates and prescribes.

If you dear reader, are a physician, you need to cancel that pact you made in the name of Jesus Christ and turn your career over to the eternal Father, the only true God, Jehova-Rophe (Jehova the Healer). This is one of His names.

---

[13] http://www.nytimes.com/2005/11/28/business/28cheer.html

Ancient Alchemy left its seeds well planted in the spiritual world. Today, even though it was transformed in its external aspect with science and materialism, in the internal, in its roots, it maintains the same goals, and the same governors. Today's pharmaceutical system continues to follow the aims of Alchemy and to be governed by Greek gods, which are none other than pagan demons.

Pharmakeia continues putting up its symbols and emblems, its serpents, caduceus, and mortars in hospitals, pharmacies, labs, and many doctors' offices and it is done with the approval from science.

In the University of Vienna, there is a painting by Gustav Klimt named *"Medicine"*. The picture presents a woman, which is none other than Hygeia, holding a bowl with a serpent engulfed in seduction, attracting humanity to death.

Hygeia "Medicine"
Picture by Gustav Klimt

4

HOW THE PHARMA-CEUTICAL INDUSTRY OPERATES

Pharmakeia is a spirit of darkness, whose purpose is to gradually enslave and kill people. In its bare form, it manifests as witchcraft and in its sophisticated and disguised form, in drugs and pharmaceutical products.

Because it is the same spirit in both forms, they operate in the same manner. The present day pharmaceutical system functions in a similiar manner to withcraft, or ancient Alchemy.

I'm not calling any physician a warlock, but do expose the system in which this spirit operates.

When somebody consults a folk healer, a witchdoctor, or a new age healer, they give the sick person a temporary solution, which has the effect of a great cure, or a supernatural miracle. This wonderous outcome raises the individual's faith in their healer, leaving them spiritually, emotionally and bodily bound to the spirit of witchcraft.

Later on, this same ENSLAVING spirit will bring another malady to the person; this one ensuring that the individual will again consult the witch doctor to perform another miracle.

Pharmakeia requires offerings and sacrifices from the person asking for consultation. None of the services rendered by

> "Pharmakeia" is a spirit of darkness, whose purpose is to gradually enslave and kill people.

Pharmakeia are free or cheap.

Medications operate in the same manner as witchcraft. They have an effect, which gives the appearance of healing, yet only the symptoms are encapsuled so the patient feels well. A series of side effects and damages, many times irreversible, accompany pharmaceutical drugs: from simple nausea, to heart attacks, terrible liver and pancreas complications, Alzheimer's, dementia, depression, memory loss, hemophilia and in some cases, even suicide.

The immunological system God created is damaged little by little, until it ends up nulllified in some cases, thereby creating one of the many forms of immunodeficiency.

Medications operate in the same manner as witchcraft. They give the appearance of healing, yet all they do is encapsulating the symptoms.

When our organs are exposed to these chemicals, they begin to cause greater health problems. Since we put our confidence in medicine, we turn to it again to acquire new medication, which continues to destroy us. In the spiritual realm, Asclepius succeeded to enslave us.

God wants to build His temple in you and Asclepius

does as well. Once the serpent has achieved the task of infiltrating its poison, the wisdom of man, "the knowledge of good and evil", celebrates and recommends it.

In Greece, there was a ritual of *"Pharmakos"* (the word for warlocks and witches) described as one entailing human sacrifices. This ritual was carried out in many cities and neighbourhoods. It was done when it became necesary to cleanse a city from the threat of plagues, pestilences, or the dangers of war and famine.

To save the majority of the population, one, or various victims whom they nicknamed *"Pharmakos"*, were sacrificed.

These individuals were treated well for a period of time and then were subsequently mistreated and murdered by the inhabitants of the area.

All the people participated in this ritual, but many sources hid the reality of those deaths.

Pharmakeia needs victims. It requires for some to die, so others can live for some time, and afterwards, die as well.

Pharmakeia demands the victims needed for laboratories. Many become guinea pigs to test their death potions. I have even seen that on North American television, as people were recruited in public to try out diverse types of medications so they can test them on human beings.

Many years ago, when I was bound to this system, I went to consult a physcian friend. While I was at his office, a pharmaceutical lab representative showed up. My friend saw him during a meeting with me, since I had his trust. I heard how the rep gave the presentation and left him a bunch of samples, so he could try them out with his patients. The catalog was full of very attractive and convincing graphics with chemical formulas and a list of benefits. Both of us looked up from the catalog and he said, *"Look what a marvel, the solution to your problem just fell in our hands."* As a parting gift, he gave me a bag full of pills and said, *"Let me know how you feel, to see if we need to increase or lower the dose."*

Innocently and blindly believing the goodwill of the pharmaceutical lab, I turned into one of their guinea pigs. And you? How many times do you think you have been used by them unknowingly?

If Pharmakeia were the solution to all our sicknesses, I would shut up and honor it. However, it is not our savior, but rather our executioner. Our real God and Savior has higher ways. Let's discover His ways together in the area of health and learn how to walk in them, and let us form a society of healthy, strong and powerful people.

Modern day medicine forms a part of a great financial control plan over humanity. An organized system, which provides billions of dollars to governments and to the mega drug industry.

Just like all the other diabolic structures, it captivates the unknowing individuals, whether physicians, or patients.

In an article published by Dr. Joseph Mercola, he states the following:

"Many times it is difficult to understand the power behind the pharmaceutical industry, yet consider this: In 2007 the global drug market was estimated at $ 693 billion dollars. It is estimated to have a $ 737 billion increase in 2008 and above $ 1 trillion for 2013.

To put these stratospheric numbers in perspective, in 2007 the pharmaceutical industry had a greater value than the total U.S. internal gross worth, which is equivalent to everything the United States produces in one year.

In 2007 the global drug market was estimated at $ 693 billion dollars. It is estimated to be above $ 1 trillion for 2013.

According to World Bank statistics, the pharmaceutical industry produced:

Belgium	**$ 448.5 billion**
Sweden	**$ 444.0 billion**
Switzerland	**$ 415.5 billion**
Norway	**$ 382.0 billion**
Saudi Arabia	**$ 381.7 million**

*When I compare the pharmacuetical industry to a gigantic money-making club, I am doing this fully intentionally. **Its power influences** governments, the manner in which conventional medicine is managed and the minds of people through massive marketing techniques unique to its sort."*

In the United States, more than fifty percent of TV commercials advertise medications. We are bombarded with the most eloquent audiovisual forms that captivate and seduce the population to aquire more and more drugs. They make up diseases of every kind, creating fear among the people. They make them believe that the minor discomfort, or symptom they are feeling, is due to a sickness that absolutely needs to be medicated. After hearing the same things hundreds of times over and over again, people begin to feel ill and start generating the symptoms these messages promote.

Dr. J Douglas Bremner wrote in his book *"Before You take that pill"*:

"The United States is the only country in the world, where you can turn on the TV and hear an advertisement which says: "Ask your doctor for this medicine." Many times doctors prescribe a medicine, which they think the patient doesn't need. For example, a study showed that in 54 percent of cases, physicians prescribe a medicine that is requested by the patient."[14]

---

[14] *Before you take that pill*, Dr. J. Douglas Bremner © 2008 Penguin Books Inc., page #11

On one occasion, a physican told me *"I no longer want to prescribe medication, but the patients get angry if I don't give them a prescription full of medicines. They tell me that the office visit wasn't worth it, unless they leave with a prescription."*

In Latin America they don't even need to consult the physician, the person attending the pharmacy is the one prescribing, and I am not tallking about the pharmacist, but the salesperson. And how does he do it? He reads the prescription the customer had brought in telling him: *"The doctor gave me this for this infirmity and said this was the best."* When the following customer comes in with the same problem, he brags about being a *"know-it-all"*, and prescribes the prescription from the previous customer." In this manner, Pharmakeia draws the victims it requires to its altar of sacrifice.

Just by hearing the numerous side effects, one can realize the solution is not there. There are cases in which the consequences of a medicine are so far-fetched that it either makes you laugh, or scares you. Such is the case with *"restless leg syndrome"*. For this new disease, they suggest medications whose side effect is *"an irresistible urge to go gambling!"*

In the United States, in 54% of cases physicians do prescribe a medicine that is requested by the patient.

This report appeared January 23ʳᵈ, 2010 in the neurology edition of the Mayo Clinic:

"A new Mayo Clinic study is the first to describe this compulsive gambling in RLS patients who are being treated with medications that stimulate dopamine receptors in the brain."

This side effect reaction, like in the cases of suicides, anger, anguish, desperation, and insanity among others, are obviously soulish and spiritual.

Dr. Mercola continues to say in his article about the pharmaceutical industry:

"What the majority of the people do not realize is the magnitude of the financial influence it exerts. That's why these corporations have blinded and deceived them, manipulating them with the false perception of "helping" humanity.

As I have demonstrated many times through the medicine lists the FDA considers high risk (and regardless of this, they continue to be sold) the pharmaceutical industry is not interested in producing elixirs and medications that aid health. On the contrary, the industry is strengthened and increases its

> The pharmaceutical industry is strengthened and increases its power, not by bringing forth a cure, but by propagating infirmity.

power, not by bringing forth a cure, but by propagating infirmity.

*Our society has turned into a **"pharmacracy"**, where at the slightest tremor or hiccup, a medication is needed.*

Inevitably, treating infirmities with medication (drugs) will bring problems later on."

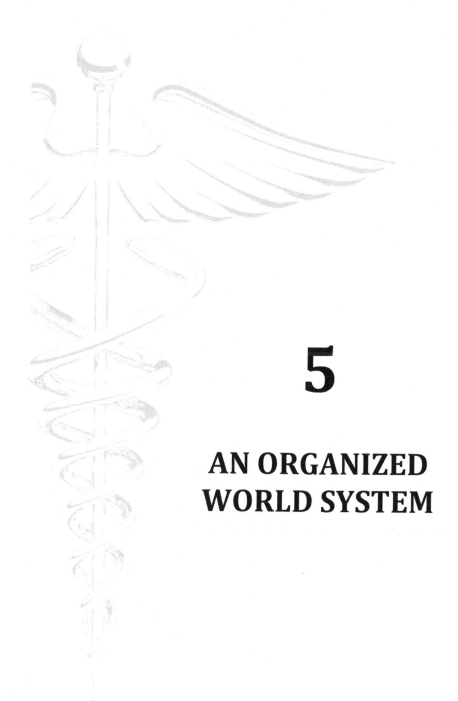

5

AN ORGANIZED
WORLD SYSTEM

Many questions arise when we deal with a subject that involves almost all of humanity. If this matter is not treated with justness, it can bring more evil than benefits. The truth is that we are living in a season where God is exposing many systems that are wrong. He is bringing the perversion and the evil that exist in the midst of our society to the light. God is a God of justice and it is under this parameter that we must analyze this delicate issue.

The questions we must ask ourselves are:

- Is the pharmaceutical system the answer to our health?

- Are the great pharmaceutical labs really interested in healing us, and once we are healed, making us stop consuming their products?

- Are the insurance companies really interested in helping us maintain health, or is it advantageous for them to have a sick society, full of fear, running to buy their insurance anticipating bad days ahead?

- What interests a medical center more: sending us home with a benign diagnosis, or creating an emergency, which leads us to an operation? How many times have you heard a doctor or surgeon say *"I recommend you get hospitalized right now, your case can't wait?"*

In former times, all babies were born at home; nowadays, the most reputable obstetricians have more cases of c-sections than of normal childbirths. As a matter of fact, they give a countless number of reasons why it's better to schedule this type of operation than to have a normal labor and delivery.

- Is it more convenient for governments to have the pharmaceutical companies sell less and pay average taxes, or is it better to create a sytem of fear and dependency, which produces billions of dollars for the labs, for the hospitals, for the government, for the insurance companies, and for the entire medical staff?

Governments are forced, by the citizens themselves, to provide medical care. The political parties know that the more they promote "better healthcare" in their campaigns, the more votes they'll have. Also, the mind set that THEY IMPERATIVELY NEED TO BE MEDICATED is deeply rooted in people's conscience. The governments know this and provide what people want, not without making sure Medicare programs only agree to pay for low quality medications.

It's all a system of vested interests. The government will supply for our "fear of death" at the lowest price possible and they will make sure people pay for the expensive medications. In this fashion, the government obtains a greater amount of taxes and with

its leftover crumbs, it supports the pharmaco-dependents, and those trapped in Medicare, or goverment health programs.

Don't think for a second that your insurance will accept a prescription for the most expensive medication on the market, or the latest discovery from Germany or Switzerland.

Senior citizens are the ones who depend mostly on the government and *Dr. Bremner* wrote this about their situation:

"A quarter of the medicines prescribed to senior citizens have a potential death risk when prescribed erroneously. The majority of the elderly are receiving drugs they do not need, or are being medicated for issues that can be treated in an appropriate form without the need of medicines."[15]

Chemicals such as acetaminophen, contained in the most popular analgesics, such as Tylenol, Anacin, Midol, Excedrin and others; is one of the medicines that mostly sends people to the hospital because of its destructive effects on the liver. Others containing ibuprofen, such as

> A quarter of the medicines prescribed to senior citizens have a potential death risk when prescribed erroneously.

---

[15] *Before you take that pill*, Dr. J. Douglas Bremner © 2008 Penguin Books Inc., page #12

Advil, Motrin, Midol-liquid gels and others; cause ulcers and bleeding in the gastrointestinal system, and have caused strokes and heart attacks. The FDA has published serious warnings against the use of these medications[16], and yet they are still on the market.

Why?

Billions of dollars and Euros form a part of the system in which us "being healthy" is not lucrative to any of the main players. It is a medical structure, which promotes infirmity; yet people view it as "God's great response" or "the benefactors of humanity".

According to statistics, 700,000 people[17] die annually in the United States due to the side effects from medicine. It is a staggering 12 million worldwide. Of the patients who are admitted into hospitals, 30 percent are due to reactions and problems caused by medications.[18]

---

12 million people die worldwide annually due to side effects of medicine.

These are the statistics that can be tracked; the numbers go sky high when it comes to the third world pharmaceutical anarchy.

Death caused by over the counter and perscription

---

[16] U.S. Food and Drug Administration (FDA) Journal on June 29th and 30th, 2009.
[17] *The Medical Mafia*, Dr. Ghislaine Lancot @ 1995 Bridge of Love Publications, U.K.
[18] *The Medical Mafia*, Dr. Ghislaine Lancot @ 1995 Bridge of Love Publications, U.K.

medication is ten times greater than that caused by illegal drugs.

In 1993, an estimated 2,216,000 patients were hospitalized in the United States for suffering severe ADR (Adverse Drug Reaction); 106,000 died, making medication the fourth cause of death in this country.

Dr. Ghislaine Lanctot, wrote a book named the "*The Medical Mafia*". It was described by *Laura Jimeno Muñoz*, the journalist from "*Discovery Health*", as the most complete, integral, explicit and clear denunciation of the role played by the complex organization formed by the Health Care System and the pharmaceutical industry.

Among the many statements she made in this book, I've extracted the following:

"It's the multinationals, the pharmaceutical companies, the ones who decide even what is taught to the future physicians in schools, what is published and what is expounded at medicine congresses! The control is absolute."

"Medicine today is controlled by insurance companies - public or private, makes no difference - because as soon as somebody has insurance they lose

> Death caused by over the counter and perscription medication is ten times greater than that caused by illegal drugs.

control over what type of medicine they access. They can no longer choose. Furthermore, insurance companies determine even the price of each treatment and the therapies to be performed. And if we look at what's behind the insurance companies, or Social Security ... we find the same thing."

"Money is what controls medicine totally and the only thing that truly interests those who manage this business, is to earn money. And how do they earn more?

Present day medicine is conceived for people to remain sick, and buy drugs, if possible, for life.

Well, making people sick ... because healthy people do not generate revenue. The strategy consists of, all things considered, having chronically sick people, who need to consume every type of palliative product, which is only to treat symptoms; medications to relieve pain, lower fever, decrease the inflammation, but never drugs that can resolve an illness. They are not interested in resolving illness, as it is not profitable. Present day medicine is conceived for people to remain sick, the longest time possible and buy drugs, if possible, for life."

1. A SYSTEM OF INFIRMITY

The so-called health care system, is in reality, a system of infirmity. A medicine of infirmity is the one practiced, not that of health. A medicine, which only acknowledges the existence of the physical body and does not take into account the spirit, or the mind, or the emotions.

In an official manner (purely illusional) the system is at the patient's service, yet in reality the system is under the industry's orders, who are the ones pulling the strings and maintaining the system of infirmity for its own inurement. It's about taking all things in consideration, an authentic "medical mafia"-system that creates sicknesses and kills for money and for power.

The physician is verily, many times unknowingly, the transmission belt for this great industry. During the five or ten years they spend going through medical school, the system takes care of instilling in them a determined knowledge, and to blind their eyes to other possibilities. They are also taught that a physician should not get emotionally attached and that he is a "god of health."

Dr. Lanctot denounces this true mafia in which all health care systems are involved. She writes:

"The medical mafia, in different levels and by different implications of course, is made up of the pharmaceutical industry, the political authorities, the great labs, the hospitals, the insurance companies, the medication agencies, the board of medicine, the physicians themselves, the World Health Organization (WHO), the United Nations, Ministry of Health - and of course, the world governments under the shadow of money.

It's a mafia that has eliminated all competition. Today, the investigators are "oriented", dissidents are put in jail, hands tied and reduced to silence. "Alternative" physicians are branded as "quacks" and their licenses are taken away, or they are also put in jail. Profitable alternative products have equally fallen into the hands of multinationals, thanks to the regulations from the WHO (World Health Organization) and the patents of the World Commerce Organization. Authorities and their social media, take charge of feeding into the population's fear of sickness, of growing old, and of death. As a matter of fact, the obsession to live longer, or simply to survive, has made the international trafficking of organs, and of blood and human embryos prosper. And in reality, in many fertility clinics, a multitude of embryos are "manufactured", which are then stored to be utilized in cosmetics, in rejuvenation treatments, etc. This is without counting the radiating of food items, gene modification, contaminated water, poisoned air. Furthermore, children absurdly receive up to 35 vaccines even before attending school."

When Dr. Lanctot was interviewed by Discovery, she said the following regarding cancer:

"The so called, so to speak massive anomalous proliferation of cells, is something so habitual that all of us suffer from it various times throughout our lifetime. But when that happens, the immunological system acts and destroys the cancerous cells. The problem arises when our immunological system is weak and cannot eliminate them; Then the group of cancerous cells ends up growing and forming a tumor.

When a tumor is discovered, the patient is immediately offered, as a pretext to help him, to choose between three possibilities or "forms of torture": amputate (surgery), burn him (radiotherapy) or poison him (chemotherapy); hiding from him that there are remedies which are effective, innocuous and cheap. After four decades of "intensive battles" against cancer, what is the situation in the industrialized countries themselves? That the cancer mortality rate has increased. That simple fact puts into evidence the failure of its prevention and treatment. Thousands of millions of Euros have been squandered, and the number of sick people, as well as the death toll, continues to increase. Today, we know who this situation benefits, we know who has created it and who supports it.

In the case of war, we all know that it benefits the weapon manufacturers and traffickers. Well, in medicine, those who benefit are the manufacturers and traffickers of the 'weaponry against cancer'; that is to say, those who are behind chemotherapy, radiotherapy, surgery, and the whole hospital industry."

One thing which really caught my attention, was an experience that happened when we were praying during an intercession strategy over the River Rhine in Germany. At the edge of this river can be found a variety of the most important pharmaceutical companies in the world. I was making prophetic declarations, delivering millions of captive people from Pharmakeia, when the Holy Spirit powerfully filled me, and through my mouth declared: *"I take authority and destroy all the substances that are being put in medications to affect human genes and convert people into homosexuals."*

We were all stunned upon this declaration, which had never, ever crossed our minds.

Further along in my investigations, I discovered that in 1973 Paul Berg and other biochemical leaders revealed the general principles of a new science: "Genetic Engineering".[19]

In 1974, the transmission of hereditary genes becomes a success. [20]

It is interesting to note that it is precisely in the seventies when the sexual revolution began and from thereon, the evermore accelerated proliferation of homosexualism.

Of course, I am not making this statement as something that is a proven fact. I place it on the table for your perusal. You discern if what I received from the Spirit may or may not be true (Try all prophesy).

Quench not the Spirit. Despise not prophesyings. Prove all things; hold fast that which is good.

1 Thessalonians 5:19-21

---

[19] *The Medical Mafia*, Dr. Ghislaine Lancot @ 1995 Bridge of Love Publications, U.K., page 148
[20] *The Medical Mafia*, dito

2. The World in Contradiction because of Vaccines

A great controversy has risen over all vaccines, which I consider worthy to be analyzed and weighed so each person makes a decision with understanding and responsibility. Ignorance is one of our greatest enemies, which can end up costing us a whole lot. In the book *"Medical Nemesis - The Expropriation of Health"*, Ivan Illich describes the diseases produced by the medical system. These carry the name of *iatrogenic*. In his study he states:

"Medicine, not content with removing from their patients consciousness the true meaning of sickness and pain, sickens them even more.

I cannot stop thinking about the vaccines which destroy children's defense systems. Many times, close to twenty are given to them before they begin their school years and then afterwards we ask ourselves why they repeatedly suffer from ear infections, which they treat with antibiotics. Later on, these same children will develop, due to these vaccines; allergies, cancers, multiple sclerosis, AIDS, etc. The list of diseases is gigantic in a population whose immunological system has been damaged.

It's interesting to note that all the vaccines first appeared after the great epidemics, which have already dissappeared in a natural manner. The perils of these vaccines are rarely mentioned unless they cause a heavy reaction after being administered." [21]

---

[21] *Medical Nemesis - The Expropriation of Health*, Ivan Illich, © 1982 Pantheon Publishers

Dr. Lanctot writes about the horrors arising from the vaccines:

"In a drastic manner, vaccines decimate the population in third world countries and chronically in the industrialized ones. To this regard, Robert McMara, the ex-President of the World Bank, former Secretary of State of the United States who ordered the massive bombarding of Vietnam and member of the expansive Immunization Program, made some shocking statements. They were denounced in a French publication named "J'ai tout compris." Here is what he said:

"We must take Draconian measures in regards to the reduction of the population against the will of the people. It has been proven that reducing the birth rate is not working, or it is not enough, therefore we must increase the mortality rate. How? Through natural causes such as "famine and diseases.""22

> Vaccines drastically decimate the population in third and first world countries.

With the fear that has cropped up over the *"Swine Flu"*, I ran into a sizeable amount of studies and publications, which denounced the seriousness of the supply and application of vaccines.

These investigations have brought the "Spanish Influenza" to light. It is worthy to analyze since it

---

22 *The Medical Mafia*, Dr. Ghislaine Lancot @ 1995 Bridge of Love Publications, U.K., page 131

undoubtedly is one of the epidemics that has caused the most deaths in history. It appeared in 1918 and practically spread throughout the whole world. It has been calculated that a third of the world's population, that means 500 million were infected and between 50 to 100 million died from it.

The majority of the victims were between 20 and 40 years of age. One of the survivors of this epidemic, Dr. Eleanora McBean ascertained that this did not come from a terribly contagious *"assassin virus"*, but from the worldwide vaccination program, which took place during the first World War. She carried out an investigation in which she demonstrated that only those who were vaccinated, died of influenza. She wrote:

"My family refused to have any vaccine administered and we enjoyed good health. One cannot contaminate our bodies with all types of poisons without these leading to infirmities. When the influenza was at its pinnacle, everything was closed down, schools, businesses, and even hospitals, since the physicians and nurses who had been vaccinated also suffered from the illness. Nobody walked down the streets, everywhere it looked like a ghost town.

It seemed that the only family that was not infected was ours, therefore my parents did what they could to help people since there were no physicians available. My parents spent hours every day caring for the sick. Had there have been a possibility of transmission, they would

have caught it. Any bacteria, germ, or virus had a great opportunity to attack them.

They never brought the disease home to infect us and we were in the middle of winter with snow everywhere.

Those of us who refused the vaccines, escaped the influenza and there were seven times more sick among the vaccinated soldiers, than among the civillians who did not get vaccinated."

Anne Riley Hale, who lived through that epidemic, also wrote:

"As we all know, the world has never witnessed such an orgy of vaccination and innoculation as the one carried out with the soldiers at the army camps."

The United Stated army lost more soldiers due to influenza than the war itself. Numerous sources report that from 14 to 25 different vaccines were applied to each soldier, which led to the epidemic.

The American navy records reveal that after vaccination became compulsory in 1911, the Typhoid index quickly rose, as well as from the other diseases inherent to the different vaccines. After the United States went to war in 1917, the death index due to the typhoid vaccine, reached its highest peak in the history of the army.

Patrick J. Caroll wrote in this regard: *"The deaths ocurred after the soldiers had been vaccinated in American hospitals and French camps that were very well supervised and had top hygiene."[23]*

A report from the U.S. Secretary of War, Henry L. Stimson stated that there were 63 deaths and 28,565 cases of Hepatitis after the soldiers had been vaccinated against yellow fever.

Dr. McBean would say that it was commonplace during the war to hear the expression: *"More soldiers die because of the vaccines than by the enemy's bullets."*

She also wrote: *"The situation became more critical when they were trying to fight against the symptoms of the diseases by increasing the vaccine doses. This produced a worse Typhoid virus named Paratyphoid. To counteract it, they created an even stronger vaccine, which gave way to the Spanish Influenza."*

The Spanish Influenza vaccine isn't the only one that resulted in other diseases and deaths. This is the problem thousands of physicians and investigators are now facing when analyzing the effects from the multitude of other vaccines.

Jon Rappoport is a reporter from the National Health Institute in the United States and ex-investigator of the most important pharmaceutical labs. In 2006 he held an

---

[23] Patrick J. Carroll, Lady Lane House, Waterford

interview with *"Dr. Mark Randall"* (pseudonym) a former vaccine researcher, who worked for many years in the laboratories of major pharmaceutical houses and the US government's National Institutes of Health. "Mr. Randall" upon finishing his own investigation remarked (interview excerpts[24]):

"I realised I was working in a sector based on a collection of lies ... As far as I'm concerned, all vaccines are dangerous. They involve the human immune system in a process that tends to compromise immunity. They can actually cause the disease they are supposed to prevent. ... And if it causes other diseases - ... - that fact is masked, because no one believes that the vaccine can do that."

Dr. Randall was asked during the interview:

Q: Why are we quoted statistics which seem to prove that vaccines have been tremendously successful at wiping out diseases?

A: Why? To give the illusion that these vaccines are useful. If a vaccine suppresses visible symptoms of a disease like measles, everyone assumes that the vaccine is a success. But, under the surface, the vaccine can harm the immune system itself. And if it causes other diseases—say, meningitis—that fact is masked,because no one believes that the vaccine can do that. The connection is overlooked.

---

[24] *"Vaccine Dangers and Vested Interests"* by Jon Rappoport, San Diego © Oct. 2004 – Jan 2006
http://www.nexusmagazine.com/index.php?option=com_docman&task=doc_view&gid=87

Q: It is said that the smallpox vaccine wiped out smallpox in England.

A: Yes. But when you study the available statistics, you get another picture.

There were cities in England where people who were not vaccinated did not get smallpox. There were places where people who were vaccinated experienced smallpox epidemics. And smallpox was already on the decline before the vaccine was introduced.

Q: So you're saying that we have been treated to a false history.

A: Yes. That's exactly what I'm saying. This is a history that has been cooked up to convince people that vaccines are invariably safe and effective.

The public believes that these labs, these manufacturing facilities, are the cleanest places in the world. That is not true. Contamination occurs all the time. You get all sorts of debris introduced into vaccines.

The SV40 got into the polio vaccine because the vaccine was made by using monkey kidneys. But I'm talking about something else. The actual lab conditions. The mistakes. The careless errors. SV40, which was later found in cancer tumours...that was what I would call a structural problem. It was an accepted part of the manufacturing process. If you use monkey kidneys, you open the door to germs which you don't know are in those kidneys.

I'll give you some of what I came across, and I'll also give you what colleagues of mine found. Here's a partial list:

- *In the Rimavex measles vaccine, we found various chicken viruses..*

- *In polio vaccine, we found acanthamoeba, which is a so-called "brain-eating" amoeba*

- *Simian cytomegalovirus in polio vaccine.*

- *Simian foamy virus in the rotavirus vaccine.*

- *Bird-cancer viruses in the MMR vaccine.*

- *Various micro-organisms in the anthrax vaccine.*

I've found potentially dangerous enzyme inhibitors in several vaccines:

- *Duck, dog and rabbit viruses in the rubella vaccine.*

- *Avian leucosis virus in the flu vaccine.*

- *Pestivirus in the MMR vaccine.*

Are some vaccines more dangerous than others? ... The DPT shot, for example. The MMR. But some lots of a vaccine are more dangerous than other lots of the same vaccine. As far as I'm concerned, all vaccines are dangerous.

And if you try to calculate what damage these contaminants can cause, well, we don't really know because no testing has been done, or very little testing. It's a game of roulette. You take your chances. Also, most people don't know that some polio vaccines, adenovirus vaccines, rubella, hep[atitis] A and measles vaccines have been made with aborted human foetal tissue. I have found what I believed were bacterial fragments and polio virus in these vaccines from time to time, which may have come from that foetal tissue. When you look for contaminants in vaccines, you can come up with material that is puzzling."

Dr. Jorge Carlos Miranda sheds some more light on this matter:

"On the subject of vaccination Mexico is a pioneer in implementing campaigns and universal vaccination programs since 1973, a year before the WHO did it.

Human error is inevitable in such a complex process as infirmity. The medical personnel deals with pathologies of diverse kinds and most of the time complicated ones with aggregate factors, not necessarily clinical ones.

In Mexico and in many other Latin countries, the absence of quality control is evident. Besides, the fact that we are living in this era of consumption, as well as other factors, have allowed the merchandising of medicine."

3. H1N1 Vaccine

Another vaccine that has appeared after a powerul fear campaign on behalf of the governments is the "Swine Flu".

The expert specialist in lungs, Dr. Wolfgang Wodarg of Germany stated that absolutely no investigations had been carried out about the side effects from the H1N1 vaccine. This vaccine entails a high risk for cancer and tumors since it is made from animal cancerous cells.

Dr. Wodarg considers the pharmaceutical industry responsible for provoking the fear of the epidemic of swine flu. It´s only purpose was to sell more medications and high priced vaccines.

The German magazine *"Stern"* wrote: *"Glaxo Smith Kline (pharmaceutical laboratory) has earned billions of Euros with the swine flu. Not only with the vaccine, but with medications such as Relenza. They have orders of 100 million packages with a production price of 18.24 Euros per package, which puts veritable billions in their hands."*

During the Swine Flu crisis, the United States ordered 251 million vaccinations.

The United States alone ordered 251 million vaccines, and Germany 68 million.

At the 4th International Vaccination Public Conference, various doctors gave their opinion about the perils of the H1N1 vaccine.

Barbara Loe Fisher, President of the National Vaccine Information Center on vaccination:

"Every vaccine has the risk of causing damage."

Dr. Warren Levin, member of a physcians committee:

"One of the reasons why I am here is to talk about the toxic aspect of vaccines."

Dr. Stephen Marini, PHD, DC immunologist and microbiologist:

"Vaccines are not what is recommended for your children. Today, there exist better methods of treating the infirmities these are hoping to prevent. Some of the side effects are asthma, allergies and autism."

Dr. Lawrence Palevsky, Pediatrician and member of the American Board of Pediatricians:

"What I learned in medical school concerning vaccines is not consistent nor effective. As the number of vaccines have increased, we have also seen an increase in chronic illnesses in children."

Others spoke about the dangers of polluting the blood of the patient with vaccines, about the heavy metal content in them, about the dangers of meningitis and paralysis, which can cause many other complications including death.

Dr. Lanctot, author of the book *"The Medical Mafia"* said at an interview taken by *Discovery Health*:

"The innumerable complications that vaccines cause, from minor disorders to death, are sufficiently documented; for example, **Sudden Infant Death Syndrome (SIDS)**. *That is why there are already numerous protests from specialists in the subject and there are thousands of lawsuits filed against the manufacturers. On the other hand, when the consequences of massive vaccination programs are examined, enlightening conclusions are clarified.*

First of all, vaccination is expensive and represents a cost of **one billion dollars annually to the government**. *It therefore benefits the industry; most notably, the multinational manufacturers. Besides, vaccination stimulates the immune system, the body's defense mechanism. Repeated vaccination exhausts the immune system. It gives a false sense of security and, in doing so, it opens the door wide to all kinds of illnesses. Notably, to those related to AIDS, which can only develop on ripe ground, where the immune system has been disturbed. It causes AIDS to explode. It ensures that the illness flourishes perpetually. More information: Vaccination encourages medical* **dependence** *and reinforces belief in the inefficiency of the body.*

*Even more, the most horrible aspect of vaccination is that it facilitates **targeted genocide**. It permits one to kill people of a certain race, a certain group, a certain country.*

*Vaccination serves as a form of **experimentation**, to test new products on a great sampling of a population and it is a **biological weapon** at the service of **biological warfare**. It permits the targeting of people of a certain race, and leaves the others who are close by more or less untouched. It makes it possible to intervene in the hereditary lineage of anyone selected.*

Investigations by eminent physicians indicate that the HIV virus was created while vaccination trials were being done against Hepatitis B among homosexual groups. Also, everything indicates that the African continent was contaminated in the the same manner during vaccination campaigns against smallpox. Of course, some investigators go even further and state that the AIDS virus was cultivated as a biological weapon and afterwards deliberately propagated through the vaccination of population groups they wanted to exterminate.

At the AIDS Congress held in Copenhagen in May 1992 the "AIDS survivors" asserted that the solution, AZT, proposed by scientific medicine to combat HIV, was absolutely ineffective. Today, this is beyond all doubt. Well then, I declare that one can survive

Vaccination encourages medical **dependence** and reinforces belief in the inefficiency of the body.

AIDS but not AZT. This medication is more deadly than AIDS. Simple common sense allows us to understand that it is not through immunodepressor drugs through which the immunological system is reinforced. AIDS has turned into another big business. Therefore, to combat it, is widely advertised since this brings in a lot of money to the pharmaceutical industry. It's that simple."

I could write hundreds of pages on the reports, studies, and lawsuits filed against the pharmaceutical companies, but I think that what I have denounced up to now, makes it clear that the solution is not there.

You decide!

6

THE ANSWER
IS IN GOD

THE CROSS VERSUS PHARMAKEIA

In order to break the yoke of medication and live in divine health, we must understand some spiritual principles.

The first thing we need to do, is recognize the internal strongholds, which make us depend on medicine.

Then, we have to create a new consciousness regarding the Will and the Power of God over our health.

Jesus is not only our Savior regarding sin, He is THE SAVIOR OF OUR INFIRMITIES. In the same manner we believe He can save us from hell, we have to believe He can save us from any malady or ailment.

Isaiah talks about the sufferings of Christ on the cross and each of them has a clear and specific meaning. He not only loved our soul to redeem it, but He turned Himself over to the most excruciating pain so we could be healed physically.

Surely He hath borne our griefs and carried our sorrows; yet we did esteem Him stricken, smitten of God, and afflicted. But He was wounded for our transgressions; He was bruised for our iniquities.

*The chastisement of our peace was upon Him and **with His stripes we are healed.***"

Isaiah 53:4-5

Take a moment and meditate deeply on the following scene:

Imagine for a moment, the Heavenly Father looking at His beloved Son, while his body is being brutally scourged. The cat-of-nine tails, tearing his back to shreds, the blows to his face, his falling down on the stones, while carrying the cross; the nails thrust into his hands and his feet cramped up due to pain in all his being; the crown of thorns perforating his head, the asphyxiation caused by hanging from a wooden board, the thirst, the unending agony, and finally the spear piercing his heart.

Feel in your own being, what the Father felt when, He Himself, was living in his heart how His Son was being destroyed. Jesus said: "The Father and I are one."

Consciously, deeply, feel what great love the Father and the Son felt for you, to make the decision of carrying out such a sizeable sacrifice.

Are you able to see how much God loves you and the price they paid so you could have access to a life in health? Do you realize what an impressive power is contained in those stripes?

The power of infirmity and of the spirits which sustain it, exploded into pieces at every wound that was inflicted to the body of our Lord, while hell screamed and groaned it´s relentless defeat.

When Jesus therefore had received the vinegar, he said, "It is finished": and he bowed his head, and gave up the ghost.

John 19:30

IT IS FINISHED.

Open up your spirit and receive these words in your heart.

Now, I want you to imagine an absurd scene:

The Father from Heaven is looking at one of His children sprawled out in bed, sick. Then He tells The Son: "Everything you suffered at the cross doesn't matter, science now has medication and very powerful physicians, therefore we will now send this little sick one these new resources so they praise My Name, ultimately because they don't have much faith in your sacrifice."

Selah!
(silence to meditate)

If I put on one side of a scale, the Blood of Christ and the Power of His stripes and on the other the power of pharmakeia, to your criteria, which one has more power?

Which God is more reliable to entrust life and health into his hands, Pharmakeia, or our Father God Almighty?

You may say: *"But Ana, I want to believe with all my being, but I do not have enough faith! I try, but I can't get it!"*

Let's put first things first. If you are a Christian, one day you surrrendered your heart to Jesus and believed in the salvation of your soul. Now, let's do something else. In the same manner and with the same conviction you surrendered your heart, I want you to surrender your BODY.

> ### Which God is more reliable to entrust life and health into his hands, "Pharmakeia", or our Father God Almighty?

Be determined to stop being the lord and sovereign over your body and the one who makes the decisions that affect you and make Jesus Christ the Lord over your entire organism. Pray now and possess the Word of God as the **only source** of salvation for your whole being.

*If there be dearth in the land, if there be pestilence, if there be blasting, or mildew, locusts, or caterpillers; if their enemies besiege them in the cities of their land; **whatsoever sore or***

whatsoever sickness there be: *Then what prayer or what supplication soever shall be made of any man, or of all Thy people Israel, when every one shall know his own sore and his own grief, and **shall spread forth his hands in this house: Then hear thou from heaven thy dwelling place, and forgive**, and render unto every man according unto all his ways, whose heart thou knowest; (for thou only knowest the hearts of the children of men:)*

2 Chronicles 6:28-30

Jesus left us, in the elements of the Lord's Supper, all the healing power from His stripes and from His Blood. I have discovered there is no man-made medicine that is more effective than the power of taking communion. When my body is imbalanced, because of a climate change, or due to the food or water of a country I've travelled to, I simply partake of the Lord's Supper and proclaim His power over my body.

In 2005, a tumor appeared in my womb. I could feel it, rub the area with my hands and it hurt. The first thing I did was decree that it was a liar, that its origin came from the father of lies, the devil, and was therefore illegal in the sanctuary of my body. I live in holiness and day to day I spread out in full sanctification.

I know I live by the grace of Jesus Christ, which is extended to me through faith and therefore I have been justified by God the Father. This gives me the authority, extended by God, to destroy the works of the devil. I can then order the lies of darkness to be invaded by the light of truth, which is Christ in me, and destroy them.

I know that Jesus Christ is "One Spirit" with me, since the Word of God establishes that he who has joined himself to Jesus, becomes one spirit with Him. This knowledge makes my faith grow and gives me strength to fight the works of my enemy.

I finished by partaking of the Lord's Supper and put all my faith in how the stripes of Jesus Christ could absorb the tumor. Even though my mouth was eating bread and grape juice, my spirit was absorbing the power of the stripes and the Blood of our Lord Jesus Christ. Then I comanded my spirit to invade every cell of my body with this power destroying every infirmity and ailment.

> I partake of the Lord's Supper and proclaim His power over my body.

In the case of my tumor, after two days of partaking of the Lord's Supper, it had dissappeared.

God allowed me to write a profound and revealing book about this subject called "*Eat My Flesh, Drink My Blood*". I recommend it´s reading, so you can grow in this marvelous knowledge, which is our inheritance in God.

7

GOD'S FORTIFIED CASTLE

We have seen how society, family and even the Church, have created thought and behavioral structures, which make us put our trust in the scientific medical sytem.

One of these strongholds is that we believe science is our security when it comes to the physical body. They have instilled so much fear in us that we live hanging from a string, thinking any moment we will need a physician. The insurance companies take it upon themselves to promote a network of lies and fears, which directs a great part of the world's population.

We have made a fortress out of the pharmaceutical system, a refuge to run to when we face the slightest discomfort or sickness.

*Woe to the rebellious children, saith tHE LORD, that take counsel, but not of Me; and that **cover with a covering, but not of My Spirit**, that they may add sin to sin: That walk to go down into Egypt, and have not asked at My mouth; to strengthen themselves in the strength of Pharaoh, and to trust in the shadow of Egypt! ... **For the Egyptians shall help in vain, and to no purpose**: therefore have I cried concerning this, Their strength is to sit still. ... For thus saith the Lord GOD, the Holy One of Israel; In returning and rest shall ye be saved; in quietness and in confidence shall be your strength: and ye would not. But ye said, No; for we will flee upon horses; therefore shall ye flee: and, We will* *ride upon the swift; therefore shall they that pursue you be swift.*

Isaiah 30, verses 1-2; 7 & 15-16

Egypt and the horses are a symbol of the strength of man, which in this case represents their wisdom filled with magic, which is Pharmakeia.

The covering from medical insurance, the wisdom of man and drugs, are a false protection, which ends up destroying us. It is a system of sickness and not of health.

The true covering comes from God, but we have to leave one, to enter the other. We cannot tell God: "I trust You, but regarding my health I trust what science can do for me." This doesn't work!

But without faith it is impossible to please Him. For he that cometh to God must believe that He is, and that He is a rewarder of those who diligently seek Him.

Hebrews 11:6

He is calling us to set our eyes on His House; on the spiritual Temple He has provided for us. To dwell in God is not to simply be a Christian and go to Church on Sundays. A dwelling place is our place of security where we feel safe from the outside world. It is our home in God, the place where we find refuge and peace. It's the

place where we long to live together with our beloved and delight in His presence. It's the place where we find true joy, where the table is always garnished with the abundance of His delicacies. It is the place of our intimacy with Him. It is a house built with divine material and that material is Christ Himself. It is a house of stable foundations built on Rock.

To dwell in His House implies continuous fellowship. It's to drink of His waters and live by them. I want you to read the famous Psalm 91 in the context of the health and love covenant God has made with you.

> We cannot tell God:
> "I trust You, but regarding my health I trust what science can do for me."
> This doesn't work!

He that dwelleth in the secret place of the Most High shall abide under the shadow of the Almighty. I will say of the LORD, **He is my refuge and my fortress; my God, in Him will I trust.** *Surely He shall deliver thee from the snare of the fowler and from the* **noisome pestilence.** *He shall cover thee with His feathers, and under His wings shalt thou trust; His truth shall be thy shield and buckler.* **Thou shalt not be afraid of the terror by night, nor of the arrow that flieth by day, nor of the pestilence that walketh in darkness, nor of the destruction that layeth waste at noonday.** *'A thousand shall fall at thy side, and ten thousand at thy right hand, but it shall not come nigh thee. Only* *with thine eyes shalt thou behold and see the reward of the wicked.'* **Because thou hast made the LORD, who is my refuge, even the Most High, thy habitation, there shall no evil befall thee, neither shall any plague come nigh thy dwelling.** *For He shall give His angels charge over thee to keep thee in all thy ways. They shall bear thee up in their hands, lest thou dash thy foot against a stone. Thou shalt tread upon the lion and adder; the young lion and the dragon shalt thou trample underfoot. Because he hath set his love upon Me, therefore will I deliver him; I will set him on high, because he hath known My name. He shall call upon Me, and I will answer him; I will be with him in trouble, I will deliver him and honor him. With long life will I satisfy him, and show him My salvation. Thou shalt tread upon the lion and adder; the young lion and the dragon shalt thou trample underfoot. Because he hath set his love upon Me, therefore will I deliver him; I will set him on high, because he hath known My name.* **He shall call upon Me, and I will answer him; I will be with him in trouble, I will deliver him and honor him. With long life will I satisfy him, and show him My salvation.**

Psalm 91

This Word is more powerful than any preventive medicine, or vaccine they want to inflict upon us. This Word is true and God Himself becomes a witness and swears over it certifying its effectiveness and veracity.

God's dwelling place is an unassailable Castle, it cannot be asssaulted. There is no virus, no bacteria, no sickness that can penetrate it. All these pathogen agents (diseases) are sent by the prince of darkness and regardless of how hard they try, they cannot penetrate God's fortress.

My husband and I minister in the jungles, in the most unhealthy places you can imagine and we never get vaccinated before a trip. There have been times in extreme missionary fields, where I have preferred not to look at what I am eating. By faith, I sanctify it and I KNOW THAT I KNOW that no microbe can penetrate the dwelling of God where I live in.

> God's dwelling place is an unassailable Castle, it cannot be asssaulted. There is no virus, no bacteria that can penetrate it.

Out of curiosity one day, we went to have our blood analyzed at a lab, which had a computer where one could see what is ocurring microscopically in the blood. The software made the red and white blood cells visible and the doctor analyzed it by studying the anomalies in the plasma (the liquid in which the blood cells navigate). When he saw ours, he observed that light was coming out of the plasma, which made it impossible to diagnose anything. Glory to God!

We are being converted into a reflection of our dwelling place, we are being transformed in what we believe.

The Apostle Paul profoundly understood what our heavenly dwelling place meant:

The result of being clothed by our heavely house is that mortality is swallowed up by the Life that is in Jesus.

*For we know that if our earthly house, this tabernacle, were dissolved, we have a building of God, a house not made with hands, eternal in the heavens. For in this **we groan, earnestly desiring** to be clothed about with our house which is from Heaven.*

2 Corinthians 5:1-2

Notice that Paul is not groaning to be clothed with white garments of salvation, but for his spiritual dwelling place. It says that he cries out in anguish, meaning it isn't something that comes automatically by grace. He continues saying:

*... that, being so clothed we shall not be found naked. For we that are in this tabernacle do groan, being burdened, not because we would be unclothed, but clothed upon, that **mortality might be swallowed up of life.**"*

2 Corinthians 5:3-4

The result of being clothed with our heavenly dwelling, is that everything mortal is absorbed by life. God Himself is wrapping us up as an unassailable castle, destroying everything that is mortal in us and against us.

To dwell in Him and Him in us, is our life guarantee. This implies that we can live in "True Peace", in His rest, knowing that no evil shall befall us. We do not have to live in fear of everything we hear on television and through insurance companies' advertising.

Indeed, there are accidents, but getting sick, does not have to be the fate for God's children. He promised He would be our fortified Castle:

"Thou shalt not be afraid of the terror by night, nor of the arrow that flieth by day, nor of the pestilence that walketh in darkness, nor of the destruction that layeth waste at noonday."

If we live in rigtheousness and covered by our God, our destiny will not be the same as those who walk in their own ways.

If we live in rigtheousness and covered by our God, our destiny will not be the same as those who walk in their own ways.

Jesus answered and said unto him, If a man love Me, he will keep My words; and My Father will love him, and We will come unto him and **make Our abode with**

him. *He that loveth Me not, keepeth not My sayings. And the Word which you hear is not Mine, but the Father's which sent Me.*

John 14:23-24

The abode is not established because we say *"Lord Lord, come and live in my heart."* First, we establish the covenant we have with Him and then, His abode built within us.

"My little children, over whom I travail in birth again **until Christ be formed in you..."**

Galatians 4:19

Begin a powerful crusade in your life until you intensely live with the abode of God inside of you and you shall see that evil will never again touch you.

We know that whosoever is born of God sinneth not, but he that is begotten of God keepeth himself, and that wicked one toucheth him not.

1 John 5:18

We may come across difficult circumstances, go through valleys of shadows and death with the purpose of growing and maturing in God and in His authority, but we will never remain prostrate.

154

8

THE TREE
OF LIFE
&
THE WISDOM
OF GOD

As we have seen up to now, scientific medicine is not the solution to living a healthy life. God wants you to be healthy and Jesus gave His life for it. He has wisdom and methods, which are higher and more effective than those men may offer.

*Behold, I will bring it **health and cure**[25]; and I will cure them and will reveal unto them the abundance of peace and truth.*

Jeremiah 33:6

We see in this scripture, how God Himself has medicines and wisdom to cure.

In the description of the Heavenly City Jesus Christ gives John in the book of Revelation, we see the Tree of Life is for the healing of the nations.

*And he shewed me a pure river of water of life, clear as crystal, proceeding out of the throne of God and of the Lamb. In the midst of the street of it, and on either side of the river, was there the tree of life, which bare twelve manner of fruits, and yielded her fruit every month: and the leaves of the tree were for **the healing of the nations**.*

Revelation 22:1-2

---

[25] **Strong's 4832. {marpe}**, *mar-pay';* from 7495; properly, curative, i.e. literally (concretely) a medicine, or (abstractly) a cure; figuratively (concretely) deliverance, or (abstractly) placidity:—((in-))cure(-able), healing(-lth), remedy, sound, wholesome, yielding.

Jesus Christ restored at the cross, the Way to Eternal Life and the access to the Tree of Life in the Kingdom of God. The true Church is the Heavenly City. This one is not in Heaven, waiting for us to die, we are the Jerusalem of the Spirit.

> *For this Hagar is Mount Sinai in Arabia and answereth to Jerusalem as it is now, and is in bondage with her children. But the Jerusalem which is above is free, and is the mother of us all.*
>
> *Galatians 4:25-26*

> *But ye are come unto mount Sion, and unto the city of the living God, **the heavenly Jerusalem**, and to an innumerable company of angels*
>
> *Hebrews 12:22*

The Tree of Life is Jesus the Messiah and its leaves, a symbol of covering and of splendor, which is also His Wisdom.

The lofty and perfect wisdom, which leads us by the hand to perfection in spirit, soul **and body.**

The Tree is at the center of the city, symbolyzing the position that Christ should occupy in our lives. The center means a place of government and authority. The city is analogous to the paradise, which is the place of our perpetual provision and from where we are blessed to have dominion.

It is also planted on one side and the other of the River of God, which is the Fountain of Life, the presence of the Most High. The Tree makes healing flow through the waters, like the heart is connected to the circulatory system, distributing life to the whole body. Likewise, the waters carry the provision of health, starting from the spirit of man, to the whole organism.

The Tree of Life is active as long as we prevail in our first love. Love is the health that flows from the tree.

Nevertheless I have somewhat against thee, because thou hast left thy first love ... To him that overcometh will I give to eat of the tree of life, which is in the midst of the paradise of God.

Revelation 2:4; 7b

The doors which give access to its leaves and to its fruit, are the obedience to God, to honor Him as God and live in holiness and thanksgiving.

The health of our bodies depends on which tree we choose to eat from, the tree of the knowledge of good and evil or from the tree of life.

Asclepius's serpent is coiled around the tree of knowledge, calling you to make him sovereign over your body and afterwards, destroy you.

The Tree of Life is the wisdom of God, which is at your disposition to live in health and in provision.

Throughout the Bible, we see God bringing words of wisdom to His people and solutions to their health. The Tree of Life is accessible when we run to it.

God showed the people of Israel what they should, or should not eat to preserve their bodies healthy. And although God cleansed all the animals, it doesn't mean they are good for our health. If we "must" eat them under a circumstance beyond our will, we do not offend God. We are not under the law, but under grace. But if we have the possibility to choose, let us elect what is good for our bodies. I will talk about this in the next chapter.

> Behold, I will bring it health and cure; and I will cure them and will reveal unto them the abundance of peace and truth.
> Jeremiah 33:6

God spoke to His prophets with specific instructions on how to cure certain diseases.

His methods are not ones from science, they are divine instructions, which when obeyed, loose the power of God over the sick one. Many of them are strange, but they are all effective.

Such is the case of Naaman's leprosy. God gives Elisha the solution and upon obeying it, the Syrian General is healed.

And Elisha sent a messenger unto him, saying, Go and wash in Jordan seven times, and thy flesh shall come again to thee, and thou shalt be clean. ... Then went he down, and dipped himself seven times in Jordan, according to the saying of the man of God: and his flesh came again like unto the flesh of a little child, and he was clean.

2 Kings 5:10; 14

Another case is King Hezekiah's infirmity, healed by the instructions the prophet Isaiah received from God.

Turn again, and tell Hezekiah the captain of my people, Thus saith THE LORD, the God of David thy father, I have heard thy prayer, I have seen thy tears: behold, I will heal thee: on the third day thou shalt go up unto the house of THE LORD. ... And Isaiah said, Take a lump of figs. And they took and laid it on the boil, and he recovered.

2 Kings 20:5;7

We see the same when Timothy is sick to his stomach.

Drink no longer water, but use a little wine for thy stomach's sake and thine often infirmities.

1 Timothy 5:23

God has taught me to run to the Tree of Life and seek first His wisdom. And this has given me extraordinary results.

When facing any symptom, we first need to find the peace and the voice of God; there in intimacy, His instructions are clearly heard.

The symptoms are only the voice of the body announcing an attack. The devil then uses fear and our mental structures, to take us into servitude and make us surrender to infirmity.

Symptoms are only the voice of the body announcing an attack. The devil then uses fear and our mental structures to drag people into slavery.

That is the moment to choose between the two trees.

The common thing is to run to the medicine cabinet and take what we think can remove that discomfort. If this perseveres, we run to the physician and we surrender to his diagnosis.

"STOP!, SAYS THE LORD:

Stop right there, I have better solutions."

1. THE WISDOM IN THE TREE OF LIFE

a.) Advice on the Spiritual end

- Check the condition of your soul and ask forgiveness for your sins. Cast away every work of the flesh that is operating in your life, or that is hidden for having been active in the past. The works of the flesh are:

Now the works of the flesh are manifest, which are these; Adultery, fornication, uncleanness, lasciviousness, Idolatry, witchcraft, hatred, variance, emulations, wrath, strife, seditions, heresies, Envyings, murders, drunkenness, revellings, and such like: of the which I tell you before, as I have also told you in time past, that they which do such things shall not inherit the kingdom of God.

Galatians 5:19-21

- Begin to manifest the fruits of the Spirit. If you do not have the Holy Spirit indwelling in you, ask the Father to give Him to you.

But the fruit of the Spirit is love, joy, peace, longsuffering, gentleness, goodness, faith, Meekness, temperance: against such there is no law. And they that are Christ's have crucified the flesh with the affections and lusts. If we live in the Spirit, let us also walk in the Spirit.

Galatians 5:22-25

Once these things are in order, rise up and fight for your health with courage and with full confidence in God.

- Resist every symptom, because it is a dart from darkness.

  Submit yourselves therefore to God. Resist the devil, and he will flee from you.

  James 4:7

- **Begin by taking authority, recognizing the Power of Jesus Christ, which abides in you, Say "No!" to the devil and to the symptom.**

- Order every lying spirit of infirmity to come out of your body in the Name of Jesus Christ.

- Do not receive it. It is a lying symptom and it is illegal in your body. You are the temple of God.

People get sick for the same reason they sin. They succumb, or they may surrender to the suggestions of the wicked one until they take possession of their hearts. Therefore, when the suggestiveness of the infirmity approaches in any form, or manifestation, you must cast it out, the same way everything that comes from the devil needs to be cast out.

Order every lying spirit of infirmity to come out of your body in the Name of Jesus Christ.

For example, how would you feel if, when you arrive at your new house that cost you thousands of dollars, you encountered the stench of dead and putrid animals?

This is an analogy to our body when we allow unclean or death thoughts (those not arising from faith) not only to live there, but to become putrid sores in us. Cancer, heart issues, blood diseases, and death are all the products of our impure, death thoughts. All of them are the products of our mental and spiritual condition, which has been formed through fear, mental structures, guilt, iniquity, curses and **unbelief.**[26]

- Ask for wisdom and God will give you the remedy.

If any of you lack wisdom, let him ask of God, who giveth to all men liberally and upbraideth not, and it shall be given him.

James 1:5

Sometimes He will tell you something as simple as: *"drink water."* Water's life-giving and healing power is impressive. The colloquial saying: "Water is Life" is not said in vain. A great amount of maladies are cured with simple water.

Exhange all your organs and bodily systems for those of Jesus.

---

[26] *Supernatural Believing*, Christ Conscious, Emerson Ferrell ©2006, www.voiceofthelight.com

In other cases He tells you, *"you are lacking in potassium, eat tomatoes."* In others He will instruct you to rest or He will give you a specific direction, or an effective grandmother's remedy. Wait for it, because it will come.

- Enter into prayer and eat from the Tree of Life. On occasions I go into prayer and while being in the spirit I see myself eating from the leaves from the tree of life, and my body feels it´s effects.

- Exhange all your organs and your bodily systems for those of Jesus. Pray to God with something such as this:

    "Jesus, You gave your life for mine and your body for my health, I now give you my lungs and in turn, I receive yours."

    If you have a blood disease, exchange your blood for His and so on with each part of your body that has affliction.

- If you are struck, you fall down, get burnt from something, you feel that bronchitis is prospering, or you get a strange chest pain, before assuming the worst, say with authority: *"devil, I don't give you my hand, leg or lungs, my heart, et cetera ... you cannot touch it, I do not surrender it to you, it belongs to Jesus Christ."*

- When you feel a symptom or you feel ill, do not repeat in your mind what you are used to thinking. Neither, say to yourself, *"if I do not take some medication I am going to get worse and I may die."* Instead say this: **"The only thing that is going to happen to me is that I am going to get well** and as of this very moment I'm beginning to feel better."

We have to undersand why we find ourselves in the condition we are in and take decisive action. He who is in sin, has to leave it. He who has not gotten delivered from the iniquities of their generational line must do it. (My book *"Iniquity,"* shall be a great blessing for you to achieve it.)

- He who is believing the lies of infirmity exchange the lie for the truth. He who is under the sentencing of a medical diagnosis, switch it to God's diagnosis.

- Partake the Lord's Supper every day, so you grow in spiritual and physical fortitude.

Beloved, I wish above all things that thou mayest prosper and be in health, even as thy soul prospereth.

3 John 1:2

When you pass in front of a hospital, or you have to go into one to pay a visit, emphatically tell it: *"YOU SHALL NEVER HAVE ME and I do not receive any fowler's snare you want to entrap me with!"* Do the same thing

> Partake the Lord's Supper every day, so you grow in spiritual and physical fortitude.

when you pass in front of a drugstore. I have done this throughout the years and I know they shall never have me.

b.) Advice in the Natural

My husband Emerson has been a very powerful instrument in my life for me to live in "Kingdom Health." God has given him divine power to fast for more than 200 days per year and an impressive wisdom about how to deal with and strengthen the body.

In this section, I have inserted an excerpt from his book, *"Supernatural Believing, Christ Conscious,"* where he talks about the practical things God has shown him on what we can do to fight against sickness.

CONCEPTS ABOUT HEALTH
THAT HAVE WORKED IN MY LIFE

by Emerson Ferrell

Currently, almost everybody is addicted to a diet which is responsible for the majority of the health issues worldwide. Without any regard to the socio-economical level of each one, the habits which deal with eating the wrong type of food are the result and consequence of living in erroneous beliefs.

Many people prefer to believe in advertisements dealing with the food they need to ingest, instead of listening to the Holy Spirit. **When we consume processed foods and sugars, this pollutes our sense of taste**, begining from our childhood. Therefore, all those meals that have less attractive flavors for our palate are, in general, the ones we most require to enjoy good health.

God is concerned about your body, because it is a temporary abode from where He directs all His Kingdom affairs in our midst. He, therefore, knows what type of fuel each one needs so we can operate at our maximum capacity level. A convenient analogy to set as an example, is that of putting

> People prefer to believe in advertisements dealing with the food they need to ingest, instead of listening to the Holy Spirit.

kerosene in your automobile's tank instead of gasoline. Filling up with the wrong fuel will destroy the engine.

To allow the Holy Spirit to complete His work in our bodies, I have discovered some very simple things that are going to help us reduce our sufferings and infirmities, the ones that come from a loss in the body's equilibrium.

For example, if I have symptoms such as body pain, fever, or excessive nasal mucuos, which indicate a cold, I immediately take Vitamin C. The amount I take ranges from 5-6 grams of pure ascorbic acid and I take it every 4 hours until the symptoms have dissappeared. Too much Vitamin C can produce diarrhea, at that moment, the dose is lowered or suspended.

Through fasting, I have discovered many secrets for healing and discovered the way to Divine Health. For example, the Lord told me: "many diseases are the result of dehydration, lack of fresh air and sunlight". That's why I try to consume a gallon, that is about four litres, of water every day and I am used to walking out in the open air under the rays of the sun. The truth is, the human body will heal itself through adequate nutrition and a moderate amount of physical excercise.

Fasting is a great tool to detox your body and to obtain a spiritual cleansing. Besides, fasting allows the Holy Spirit to instruct us in the maintenance we should give His temple, which is our body, once we have ended the fast.

We have learned to eat papaya when we have a stomach ache, or any symptom such as nausea or vomiting, and green tea is better than drinking coffee.

We avoid food items having a great amount of toxins. Our bodies, as chemical organisms, were designed to eat the nutrients God designed for our health. The body does not recognize, nor does it know what to do with toxins, therefore it stores them in the lymphatic system. This is a thin small network found at the subcutaneous layer (underneath the skin) and is where the body's energy runs through, as well as the power of the anointing. If this network is obstructed by toxins, the energy will not get to where it needs to go and the power of God will be obstructed, not able to flow through your hands. Besides medicine, the most toxic food items are:

Refined sugar, bottled or canned drinks such as soft drinks, Coca-Cola or Sprite and the like, which are sheer poison to our organism.

Pork meat, shellfish and fish without scales or gills, which are bottom feeders, such as sole as well. All these feed from waste and feculence, which makes them highly toxic.

Fasting in Christ is a great tool to detox your body and to obtain a spiritual cleansing

Products containing any sort of yeast are better to be avoided.

My wife and I take nutritional supplements to balance the deficiencies of nutrients in modern day food items.

These steps are so simple, they have aided in maintaining our body, while the Holy Spirit sanctifies our being completely.

The most important thing I have learned about fasting, is that the less food I consume in the natural, the more spiritual food I will receive. The effect from this is like a waterfall, which imparts divine health to my spirit, soul and body.

Don't let the devil condemn you for using a hospital, or a doctor. For example, if somebody suffers an accident in their automobile, you must trust that the Lord will provide a doctor to be in charge of your immediate necessities. I do not recommend any type of operation, but every person has to trust Jesus according to the level their faith has taken them to.

Trust in the Holy Spirit for all your needs, especially in what relates to your health and in this manner you will be protected.

My wife and I entered into a health covenant with God and taking the words of Shadrack, Meshack and Abednego in the Book of David.

We told Him we would not bend over to Pharmakeia:

'If it be so, our God whom we serve is able to deliver us from the burning fiery furnace, and He will deliver us out of thine hand, O king. But if not, be it known unto thee, O king, that we will not serve thy gods, nor worship the golden image which thou hast set up.'

Daniel 3:17-18

Finally, you must trust in the Holy Spirit for all your needs, especially in what relates to your health and in this manner you will be protected, so you do not have any accidents. Paul was beaten, stoned and carried a goad in the flesh (*2 Corinthians 12:6;12*). The Lord told Paul that His grace was sufficient for him.

To overcome we must know the meaning that exists behind the definition of *"Unmerited Grace"*. Grace is the supernatural power of God, imparted through the resurrection of Christ Jesus, **so we can know the truth.**

'For the law was given by Moses, but grace and truth came by Jesus Christ.'

John 1:17

Truth is a person. He is Christ Jesus. The truth becomes incarnate when we come to live inside of Jesus. This is possible due to the grace He provided for us. Jesus Christ never lived in fear of accidents, or sickness, or sufferings, or of death itself. Jesus is waiting to open the door of the supernatural for you. **If you can believe in it, you can live in it.**"

2. OTHER PIECES OF ADVICE THAT WILL BE USEFUL TO YOU

The first thing we need to do to begin our walk to pharmaceutical freedom is to strengthen our organism's defense system. The simplest way is taking Vitamin C at least two grams per day. Some people tolerate more, let them do so.

Today's market offers a fair amount of products based on natural aminoacids which raise our defenses.

A change in our eating habits is paramount to having good health. Do not consume *"fast foods"* under any circumstance. Hot dogs, hamburgers from such establishments as *McDonalds* and *Burger King*. These are made with animal by-products and can contain such shocking items as worms, rats, dogs and decomposed entrails. There have been heavy lawsuits filed against these establishments, because of the level of unhealthiness of their products.

Natural News [27] published the following:

"If you're in the beef business, what do you do with all the extra cow parts and trimmings that have traditionally been sold off for use in pet food? You scrape them together into a pink mass, inject them with a chemical to kill the e.coli, and sell them to fast food restaurants to make into hamburgers.

---

[27] http://www.naturalnews.com

That's what's been happening all across the USA with beef sold to McDonald's, Burger King, school lunches and other fast food restaurants, according to a New York Times article. The beef is injected with ammonia, a chemical commonly used in glass cleaning and window cleaning products."

Many rumors have circulated that, what they use, is not even meat, but instead some worms reproduced in labs. Obviously, if this is true, it is among the company's Top Secrets. These rumors may, or may not be true. One truth is evident, there are many rumors. You decide.

Avoid oversaturated oils such as corn or sunflower oils, and margarines. Instead, use olive or canola oil. Eating greasy fried foods or deep fried foods is terrible for cholesterol and your arteries' health.

Medicines and the wrong foods may have imbalanced your organism and you need to tone it and give it nutritional supplements if they are within your economic means. If not, ingest fruits and vegetables as much as you can and maintain a balanced and healthy food intake.

Today, there are books written by expert nutritionists that can help you counteract symptoms through teas, or natural substances.

> A change in our eating habits is paramount to having good health.

God has given us, through nature, many things that can be of great benefit to us.

Herbal markets in Latin America, and often other countries alike, are controlled by witches, warlocks and folk healers. This doesn't mean that the herbs God created are evil, but that they are in the wrong hands. However, there are natural supplement laboratories which are not consecrated to the devil and you can use them. The suitable thing would be for us to have our own Christian nurseries. May God touch, who He needs to touch.

For some of the simple illnesses such as a sore throat, I put ten drops of iodine in a glass of water and take it once a day. More than that can be dangerous.

Iodide boosts the immunological system and cleanses the glands. It is excellent for thyroid and goiter problems.

The best thing for colds or the sniffles is Vitamin C and a sea water saline solution in a spray form to decongest the nasal passages.

A great amount of people suffer from insomnia due to the stress in our society and as a side effect from some medications. Valerian, melatonin, chamomille tea, linden, orange blossom, or mint will help you sleep. Try to pray, read, or do something that relaxes you two hours before you go to sleep. Try not to think of everything you have to solve the following day, because that will take your sleep away.

Casting all your cares upon Him, for He cares for you.

1 Peter 5:7

For the heart, a couple of dark chocolate squares are quite effective.

There are many natural solutions and there are expert nutrionists for this, along with alternative medicine physicians (not New Age) from where you can obtain good advice.

In his commentary for this book, Dr. Jorge Carlos Miranda wrote the following regarding nutrition:

"The existing relationship between the process of health to infirmity and the levels of nutrition in a country have been demonstrated. First of all, the infant and pre-school mortality rates are closely related to nutrition and deficiencies in this area elevate the vulnerability to chronic ailments.

Diverse investigations have revealed that infant mortality is three times higher among people of lower income than those in the upper classes, a fact that is directly related to the nutritional conditions. This is revealing data to this regard, since it is estimated that 2 million children are presently born in Mexico annually. 100,000 die before the age of 5 and around 1 million survive with physical and mental defects due to nutritional deficiency.

According to information from the World Health Organization (WHO) chronic degenerative diseases, such as: Heart Disease, Cerebral Vascular Accidents, Cancer, Chronic Respiratory Diseases, and Diabetes, cause twice the amount of deaths for all infectious diseases. It is 35 million deaths per year presently (60%), an estimated 41 million in 2015, a 17% increase.

The causes for the main epidemics of chronic diseases are well established and are well-known:

1. Unhealthy diet. Around 17 million, or 30% of total global deaths from cardiac diseases/CVD and Strokes are caused by bad nutrition. For cancer, dietetic factors represent 20–30% of the factors for all types of cancer; currently 20 million suffer from it, a 30 million people increase is estimated in 20 years. Diabetes is considered an epidemic. It causes one death every 10 seconds. 171 million persons suffer from it currently and a 350 million people increase is estimated by 2030.

The infant and pre-school mortality rates are closely related to nutrition.

A healthy organism, properly nourished, is less susceptible to bacterial, viral, parasitic and fungi infections due to the adequate response from the immunological system.

---

2. Physical Inactivity, sedentarism, other conditions for being overweight along with these, lead to the development of cardiovascular diseases and resistance to insulin.

3. Tobacco and Alcohol Consumption, which have a toxic and destructive effect, due to the generating of free radicals attacking the cells, are predisposing factors to develop cancer.

The Main Causes of diseases are:

1. Unhealty Diet

2. Physical inactivity

3. Tobacco & Alcohol Consumption

We must add to this the impact from the industrialization of food processing, environmental pollution through factories, automobiles, pesticides, radio-frequencies, among others. There is an article about the impact of the four deadly whites (salt, sugar, refined flours, and milk).

Some of the institutions at a worldwide level such as: The World Health Organization, CDC, American Heart Association, National Cancer Institute, U.S. National Institutes of Health, American Diabetes Association and National Diabetes Education Program tell us that the main preventive measures to avoid the development of chronic-degenerative diseases, are: the consumption of whole grains, fruits, vegetables, and fish, as well as routine physical exercise to maintain a healthy weight."

9

HOW TO INCREASE OUR FAITH TO STOP TAKING MEDICINE

MIRACLES AND DIVINE HEALING

Testimony by Emerson Ferrell

"**D**ivine Healing" consists in removing the infirmities through the power of God. It's the life of God transmitted to our being, rather coming directly from Heaven, or through another man or woman of faith. Divine Health consists of living day after day, and hour after hour, in contact with God, so the life of God flows into our body in the same manner it flows into the mind or into the spirit.

A miracle is a creative act from the Spirit of God. In order to impart healings and miracles to these clay beings (us), the Holy Spirit blows His life into the dying areas of our bodies. The more we believe in the invisible, the greater the result will be.

Our actions and trust in God determine our healing. Once salvation begins in our spirit, nothing, abolutely nothing has the power to stop His virtue, except our refusal to believe.

It doesn't matter how cute our lamps are if they don't produce any light. If the fuses are blown and there is no electricity running through the cables, the result is no light. Our spirit works the same way. The Holy

> "Our actions and trust in God determine our healing."

Spirit is the power from heaven, who invests us with virtue and faith. Unbelief manifests as blown fuses.

When the Holy Spirit connects to our being, this is equivalent to going from a 110 volt current to a more powerful 220 volt. Power is not only duplicated but it increases incredibly, at a fantastic speed, frequency and quantity.

Faith that impregnates all your being feels like lightning inside your body. I have been able to experiment with this sensation on various occasions and everytime my faith knows no limits. I feel like if I could believe anything, it will turn into reality. This is the connection of the Holy Spirit to all our being. Jesus maintained that power, due to the unity He had to His Father and to the Holy Spirit.

True healing has a progressive development. Once the spirit of man has connected to the virtue of God, our responsibility consists in taking it very seriously.

At that point, our spirit should not rest until the Holy Spirit consumes in us every thought of illness, symptoms and defeat.

> "True healing has a progressive development."

At the moment you begin to set your priorities in order and eat of His Word, your spirit will begin to fill up with power.

My life changed

dramatically when I found out my soul and my body were in a state of spiritual anemia. I began to fast, first only from solid foods and began to feed myself with spiritual food all day long. Sometimes this would last until the dawn hours of the following day. The first thing I did was read the Bible from Genesis to Revelation. My encounters with the Holy Spirit changed from being occassional to becoming constant. His voice became clearer and stronger until the voices of doubt and unbelief ended up being practically mute.

My spirit was gaining authority over my mind and over my body. I substituted the images of fear and skepticism I previously had with a type of knowledge that I cannot even describe with words. The invisible became visible, as I spoke.

For example, my son was suffering from an ear infection and his temperature was running very high. I could see myself right there standing in his bedroom, but I was much taller than what my real height is. When I went into his room, the spirit that was over my son began to tremble in terror.

I told it: *"You filthy spirit, leave my son's body at this instant!"* Before I finished the phrase the foul spirit left, and my son's temperature immediately returned to normal.

"Spend time in the Word of God. Spiritual food is vital to be able to have strength and revelation."

Since then, I have been very diligent in practicing various things. First, every day I spend time in the Word of God. Spiritual food is vital to be able to have strength and revelation. Revelation is the greatest proof that you have contact with the Holy Spirit.

It is of utmost impotance that you surround youself with true believers and that you partake of the blessings the Lord gives you. The Holy Spirit needs a human voice to tell the rest about His nature and His character. Therefore, if you become a living testimony, who talks about His wonders, your faith will grow and will inspire many.

The point I am trying to affirm is that our healing is as sure as our salvation. However, we are not going to receive what Jesus bought for us, if our belief system turns into doubt and unbelief. It's like somebody who has a million dollars in the bank, but can't even withdraw one penny because of his unbelief.

If your spirit is in the position where it has no appetite for spiritual things, you will be an easy target for the devil. You will not have the physical healing you need until you receive spiritual healing. If you obtain your healing through the Spirit and you maintain your connection vibrant and fresh through the steps we have explained, you will live in divine health and never in

"Become a living testimony and your faith will grow."

your life will you need help from doctors in regard to ailments or disease.

Once you have joined and converted into one with Christ Jesus, in spirit, soul and body; infirmity will fall off your body in the same manner the scales fell off Paul's eyes.

The Mind of Christ will not allow anything impure to prosper in your life.

"Our healing is as sure as our salvation."

As a matter of fact, nothing from this realm will be able to come close to you. Nothing shall approach you unless your spirit weakens. Keep your spirit strong and your soul, and your body will live in complete "Divine Health".

CONCLUSION

Taking the step to leave scientific medicine will be different for each person.

Not everybody has the faith to throw out their medications in the garbage and never again depend on them. To do this, a strong conviction and leading from the Holy Spirit are needed.

For others, it will be a gradual path according to their state of health and their level of faith.

When you learned to walk, you fell a couple of times, which is normal. Some decide to leave their medicines and when the struggle becomes too hard, they go back to taking them again, or find themselves going to the hospital. Don't feel condemned because of that. Regain your strength and set out again on the path to victory. **Convince yourself that you will accomplish it one day.** Many have already done it and there is no reason for you to accept defeat. You are more than a conqueror.

"The key is to have science serving us, instead of being under it's yoke."

If you have to take a medicine or consult a physician, let it be your last option and not the first.

Before taking a medication, investigate the health risks it may have. The internet has a multitude of sources listing the side effects and health risk associated with medications. Remember, there are some that have been banned and are still on the market, such as *Tylenol* and *Advil*.

(Liver toxicity from acetaminophen poisoning is by far the most common cause of acute liver failure in the United States, researchers reported)[28].

There are occasions when it will be necessary for some of you to go to a hospital, because of an emergency or

---

[28] By Neil Osterweil, Senior Associate Editor, MedPage Today, published Nov. 30th, 2005
Reviewed by Robert Jasmer, M.D.; Assistant Professor of Medicine, University of California, San Francisco.

an accident. Of course in these situations, go and let the physicians save your life.

The key is that we are not under the yoke of Pharmakeia, yet science can be at our service when we need it. She serves you, not the other way around.

There are occasions when you will have to get a tooth filled because of a cavity and you will have to go to the dentist. Go with confidence. When I have to go get a cleaning or a molar filled I do it but I do not take "preventive medicine" or anesthesia.

One day I had to go in for a very painful teeth cleaning and the Holy Spirit told me: *"Ask Me for an Anesthesia Angel."* I was surprised, but I did it. During the procedure, an angel was next to me with his finger of light over my teeth. I did not feel any pain and I was able to preach about the supernatural power of God to the whole medical office.

God is giving you light in these pages and showing you the exit door. Each one shall exit at their pace and in their time. God does not condemn anyone for taking medication, but I want to take you to a higher path and offer you the health He paid the price for at the cross.

FINAL PRAYER

"Heavenly Father, I pray for all those who have read this book and yearn to be free from the power of Pharmakeia. I rebuke and immobilize the spirit of sorcery in the drugs. I order the powers of alchemy and those of the gods Asclepius, Pharmakeia, Hygeia, Hermes, Apollos and all the Greek and Egyptian gods, be broken right now in the lives of my brothers and sisters. May the destructive effect from each substance they have ingested be undone by the power of the blood of Jesus Christ.

I command all the chains that enslave them be broken and their prison doors be opened that he/she may exit right now from the slavery to Pharmakeia.

May you, Eternal Father, fill him/her up with love and peace to take the steps to their freedom. May an unbreakable conviction of faith now come upon him/her; the faith that overcomes the world and may that faith never leave them.

I thank you for the millions which shall be free and shall be filled with Your wisdom.

Receive all the honor and the glory together with your son Jesus our Messiah for the wonderful atonement, which has set us free."

PRAYER FOR PHYSICIANS

Heavenly Father, I place in your hands every physician that has read this book. I bless him/her in your Name and I thank you for their lives.

If you swore to the Hippocratic Oath, it is necessary for you to break it by the power of the blood of Jesus, since it is a pact you entered in ignorance with satan.

Say: I renounce every pact with satan, with Asclepius, with pharmakeia, with Hygeia and with all the greek gods. I renounce the Hippocratic Oath and declare that the greek gods are neither my judges nor my protectors, but you Jehova of the Hosts, the only True God. I remove the veil of darkness from my eyes that pharmakeia put over them, so as not to see the destruction this spirit is causing in people.

I ask you Lord Jesus, Physician of physicians, to raise me up in wisdom and in the understanding of your Kingdom and your paths to help out many people that need you.

I want to be an instrument of health in your hands, an instrument of life to instruct many in your paths of health and life. I want to be a Physician of Your Kingdom, so the world can see you and know you. In the name of Jesus Christ my Lord. Amen.

BIBLIOGRAPHY

The Confessions of Saint Augustine (1963),
Rex Warner, Signet/Mentor Books

The Origins of Alchemy (2001), Marcellin Berthelot P. E.

Alchemy: Science of the Cosmos, Science of the Soul (1967),
Titus Burckhardt , Fons Vitae Publishing

*The Black Arts: A Concise History of Witchcraft, Demonology, Astrology,
and other Mystical Practices throughout the Ages* (1983),
Richard Cavendish, Perigee Trade Books.

Alchemy and Chemistry in the Seventeenth Century, papers read by
Allen G. Debus & Robert P. Multhauf at Clark Library Seminar
(March 12, 1966), William Andrews Clark Memorial Library,
University of California, Los Angeles.

The Dark Side of History (1977)
Michael Edwardes, Stein and Day, New York

Encyclopedia of the Occult (1986),
Fred Gettings, Rider & Co., London

*A Chemical History Tour: Picturing Chemistry
from Alchemy to Modern Molecular Science* (2000),
Arthur Greenberg, Wiley-Interscience.

Remarks upon Alchemy and the Alchemists (1857),
Ethan Allen Hitchcock, Boston: Crosby, Nichols and Company

Medieval Europe: A Short History. 6th edition (1990),
C. Warren Hollister, McGraw-Hill College, Blacklick, Ohio

The Origins of Alchemy in Graeco-Roman Egypt (1970),
Jack Lindsay, Barnes & Noble.

On the Elements (1976), Richard C. Marius Dales,
Berkeley, Los Angeles & London, University of California Press.

Thomas Norton's Ordinal of Alchemy (John Reidy editión) (1975),
Thomas Norton, London/New York, published for Early English Text
Society (No. 272) by Oxford University Press

Robert Boyle: Father of Chemistry (1959),
Roger Pilkington,John Murray Publ., London

The World of Physics (1987),
Jefferson Hane Weaver, Simon & Schuster, Inc., New York

The Occult: A History (1971),
Colin Wilson, Random House, New York

Chemistry, 2nd edition (1989)
Steven S. Zumdahl, Heath and Co, Maryland

Comments by Dr. Jorge Carlos Miranda

La Medicina está enferma, (Medicine is Sick)
Federico Ortíz Quesada, Limusa

The World Health Organization,
Centers for Disease Control and Prevention (CDC), Atlanta, GA, USA

American Heart Association, Dallas, TX, USA
National Cancer Institute, Bethesda, MD, USA
U.S. National Institutes of Health, Bethesda, MD, USA
National Diabetes Education Program, Bethesda, MD, USA
American Diabetes Association, Alexandria, VA, USA

John G. Lake (1995), Kenneth Copeland,
Kenneth Copeland Publications, Tulsa, Oklahoma, USA

Medical Nemesis - The Expropriation of Health (1982),
Ivan Illich, Pantheon Publishers

The Medical Mafia (1995), Dr. Ghislaine Lancot, Bridge of Love Publications, U.K.

Report "*Death by Medicine*" by Gary Null, PhD, Carolyn Dean,
MD, ND Martin Feldman, MD, Debora Rasio, MD, Dorothy Smith, PhD.

Before you take that pill (2008),
Dr. J. Douglas Bremner, Penguin Books Inc

My own experience with anti-inflammatories.

Voice of The Light Ministries

Visit our website at:

www.voiceofthelight.com

Write to:
Voice of The Light Ministries
P.O. Box 3418
Ponte Vedra, FL 32004
United States of America

contact.us@voiceofthelight.com

Follow us on **Facebook** and **Twitter**. Watch us on
Frequencies of Glory TV and **YouTube**.

www.youtube.com/voiceofthelight

www.frequenciesofglorytv.com

www.facebook.com/VoiceoftheLight

twitter.com/AnaMendezF

Made in the USA
Coppell, TX
11 September 2020

37508747R00115